Advance Praise

"A stirring chronicle of the singular basketball team that made bracket-busting history and thrilled a nation."

— Hall of Fame broadcaster Jim Nantz

"What UMBC accomplished in 2018 was one of the most remarkable college basketball stories I've ever witnessed. Kevin Cowherd takes the reader inside that season with his detailed reporting right up until the 'shock and awe,' moment when the Retrievers became the first 16th-seed to EVER win an NCAA Tournament game."

— John Feinstein, #1 *New York Times* best-selling author, sportswriter and sports commentator

D1260132

U Must Be Cinderella!

U Must Be Cinderella!

Inside College Basketball's
Greatest Upset Ever and
the Audacious School
That Pulled It Off

Kevin Cowherd

Apprentice
House Press
Loyola University Maryland

First Edition

Hardcover ISBN: 978-1-62720-347-0
Paperback ISBN: 978-1-62720-348-7
Ebook ISBN: 978-1-62720-349-4

Printed in the United States of America

Design: Apprentice House
Managing editor: Danielle Como

Cover photograph by Mitchell Layton

Published by Apprentice House Press

Apprentice House Press
Loyola University Maryland
4501 N. Charles Street
Baltimore, MD 21210
410.617.5265
www.ApprenticeHouse.com
info@ApprenticeHouse.com

Contents

. . . .

This book is dedicated to underdogs everywhere.
You endlessly inspire us.

"It always seems impossible, until it is done."
— *Nelson Mandela*

"In order to attain the impossible,
one must attempt the absurd."
— *Miguel de Cervantes*

Acknowledgements

• • • •

A book that purports to be about college basketball's greatest upset ever – and, yes, that's what's being purported here – could never be written without the assistance of many others.

My thanks go out to the entire UMBC community and especially to the administration, which willingly granted me the level of access and cooperation needed for a project of this nature. I first pitched the idea for the book to school vice-presidents Greg Simmons and Lisa Akchin during a long lunch. The fact that both listened patiently without rolling their eyes or staring down at their salads suggested I might be onto something.

Retrievers head coach Ryan Odom, assistant coaches Nate Dixon, Eric Skeeters and Bryce Crawford, and players Daniel Akin, Max Curran, Nolan Gerrity, Jourdan Grant, Brandon Horvath, Arkel Lamar, Jairus Lyles, K.J Maura and Joe Sherburne could not have been kinder as I picked their brains endlessly about the magical 2018 post-season the team enjoyed.

I will also never forget how open and honest Ryan Odom, his wife Lucia, and their son Connor were in sharing the details of Connor's painful struggles with OCD. To this day, all three continue to tell the story to anyone who will listen, in the hope that it can comfort and inspire others suffering from mental distress.

I also owe an enormous debt of gratitude to Dr. Freeman A. Hrabowski III, UMBC's gregarious president and the school's foremost evangelist, who was a big booster of this book from the beginning. He was also an especially valuable source of information on how the Retrievers' historic win over Virginia affected the university emotionally and financially in the weeks and months that followed.

I'm also honored that he was willing to share many of the intimate and harrowing details of his life growing up in segregated Birmingham, AL in the 1960's. Despite the enormous challenges he faced then and in his early academic career, I have never seen Freeman without a smile on his face. You wonder if the man has ever had a grouchy day in his life.

Thanks also go out to the terrific announcing team of Jim Nantz, Bill Raftery, Grant Hill and Tracy Wolfson for taking me behind the scenes of TBS' broadcast of the historic UMBC-Virginia game, as well as the truTV telecast of UMBC-Kansas State two days later.

Zach Seidel, UMBC's young and talented digital media director, also deserves a shout-out and praise for explaining to this Boomer author – again and again, with infinite patience—how the @UMBCAthletics account became the talk of the Twitterverse, as well as the rest of social media, during the Retrievers epic March Madness of three years ago.

Others who graciously offered their assistance in the crafting of this book include: David Castellanos, Brandon Gehret, Sarah Hansen, Garrett Hasken, mascot performer extraordinaire Cara Jaye, Corey Johns, Alexander Jones, Nick Kelly, Leslie Kruger, Zac McCord, Ronny Meghairouni, Dave Odom, Patrick Ogoh, Zoe Pekins, Dave Robinson, Kim Robinson, first-reader extraordinaire Bill Rose, Laura Schraven, Mike Spano, Dinah Winnick, and James Wiggins.

A shout-out and special thanks also go out to my buddies and former Baltimore Sun colleagues John Eisenberg and Dan Rodricks, for all their advice and encouragement with this and other projects.

Special thanks are also owed to my friend Kevin Atticks, the unflappable publisher at Apprentice House Press. This is the fifth book we have done together. I could pick up the check a hundred times when we meet for beers and wings and still not come close to repaying him for all the support he's given me through the years.

Finally, I am indebted most of all to Steve Levy, UMBC's veteran SID and all-around good guy, without whom this project would have floundered big-time. For months and months, Steve took my calls at all hours of the day and night and never complained when I swamped him with text messages and emails seeking information.

As a 1985 UMBC grad who has worked at his alma mater ever since, his exhaustive knowledge of its inner working and its sports team proved to be invaluable. Tirelessly, he suggested sources, arranged interviews (in-person and via Zoom), tracked down photos and provided context for the events that took place over an enchanted March weekend in Charlotte, N.C., when the Retrievers made basketball history and thrilled the nation.

Thanks for everything, Steve. You're the best.

CHAPTER 1

"Are You Guys Even D-1?"

• • • •

Charlotte, N.C.

Jairus Lyles is the one who puts it in perspective, who tries to calm any jitters in his UMBC teammates.

All week in practice, as the Retrievers prepare to face powerful Virginia in the first round of the 2018 NCAA basketball tournament, the senior guard keeps saying: "Yo, it's not like we're playing the Monstars."

It's the perfect line for the occasion. They all loved the "Space Jam" movie as kids. So the reference to the hulking, snarling cartoon villains who steal the talents of a bunch of NBA All-Stars to make themselves into an invincible super-team resonates in a big way.

"It's basketball," Lyles reminds the Retrievers. "We've been playing it all our lives. This is just another game."

Each time he says it, point guard K.J. Maura can feel everyone on the team getting more and more energized.

When your captain and your main guy says that, Maura thinks, *it's like: He believes! So we all gotta believe! We have no choice!*

Except now, as the no. 16-seed Retrievers take the court for warm-ups on this unseasonably warm March evening before their game against the no. 1 overall seed Cavaliers, it's clear there are few other believers here in Spectrum Center.

Oh, shoe-horned into a couple of sections, one court-side and the other high in nosebleed territory, the 500 or so Retrievers fans in their black-and-gold gear leap to their feet and cheer raucously. The band launches into the stirring fight song "UMBC Riser" and True Grit, the Retriever mascot, struts about as the cheerleaders clap along in a syncopated rhythm that makes the whole thing sound like an unholy battle hymn.

But as they break into lines for layups, the Retrievers sense quite a different vibe from the sea of Virginia fans that have made the four-hour trip down from Charlottesville.

Smiling and chatting quietly among themselves, arms folded contentedly across their chests, they could pass for a polite opera crowd waiting for the curtain to go up if not for all the navy and orange swag.

Look at them! Maura thinks. *They're not worried about us at all! It's like they're gonna blow us out by 50!*

The Retrievers are used to this kind of disrespect. They play for a mid-sized university outside Baltimore that 90 per cent of hoops fans have never heard of, one still tagged – erroneously – as a "commuter school," that dreaded pejorative that signals a social life gulag. It's a school where the big source of athletic pride is the chess team, for God's sake, with six national titles.

Then again, this is what happens when your basketball team flat-out stinks for years, when it had eight losing seasons in a row and just 41 wins over that stretch until recently.

Especially when they go up against a snooty Power Five school, the Retrievers know the condescending questions will come hard and fast: "UMBC? What's that? Are you guys even D-1?"

If they're in a decent mood, Maura and his teammates will patiently clue people in on the University of Maryland, Baltimore County. "We're a science, tech and engineering school," they might say. "Highly-selective, too. Sure, we're D-1 in athletics. But there're no dumb jocks here, bro. The mop guy who wipes the floor during games probably has a Ph.D."

Maura and Co. could point out that famous alums include the actress Kathleen Turner, the superstar pastry chef Duff Goldman, and the U.S. Surgeon General Jerome Adams. But that's unlikely to impress their smirking opponents or end their snarky interrogations.

If they get pissed at all the dumb questions, though, the Retrievers will simply glare and walk away and use the slight as motivation. Which is why they so often seem to be playing this season with a chip on their shoulders the size of a sequoia.

Of course, ignorance of their opponent aside, there are plenty of reasons for Virginia fans to feel smug in the moments before this 9:40 p.m. tip-off in the second game of the South Regional.

With a flashy 31-2 record, the Cavaliers are having a season for the ages. They're the best team in college basketball, no. 1 in the AP poll for the first time since December of 1982. They're also the first ACC team to win 17 conference games. Their only losses were to no. 18 West Virginia two weeks before Christmas and to Virginia Tech by a point in overtime in a nationally-televised game Feb. 10.

Yes, they're playing tonight without 6-foot-7 forward De'Andre Hunter, the ACC Sixth Man of the Year, out with a broken wrist. But that hasn't exactly caused the pundits to change their thinking about the outcome. Nor has it caused any of the smart money to jump on UMBC.

The Vegas bookmakers still list the 24-10 Retrievers as 20 ½-point underdogs. ESPN's Power Basketball Index gives them a 1.5 per cent chance of winning. And they're still a whopping 5,000-to-1 shot to make it to the Final Four in San Antonio, Texas.

This is a team ranked 188 in the Ken Pomeroy analytical/efficiency ratings. A team that lost in January by 44 points – *44!*—to that noted basketball power, Albany.

The Baltimore Sun, the Retrievers' hometown newspaper, is so convinced they'll get waxed it hasn't even bothered to send a reporter to cover the game. Which leads to the not-unrealistic prospect of UMBC fans opening tomorrow's sports section and finding the final score next to the tire ads on page 5, in a brief with the sub-headline: "In other tournament results . . .."

The Retrievers must also contend with this thoroughly depressing stat: a 16-seed has never beaten a 1-seed. Never, ever. In fact, 16-seeds are 0-135 against 1-seeds going back to 1985, when the tournament expanded its field.

The closest a 16 has come to beating a 1 was way back in 1989. That year, on a pre-game show, a young ESPN commentator named Dick Vitale promised to don a Princeton cheerleaders' outfit if the 16th-seed Tigers knocked off mighty top seed Georgetown.

"I think we're a billion to one to win the whole tournament," Princeton's colorful coach, Pete Carril, told reporters beforehand. "To beat Georgetown, we're only 450 million to one."

The game went down to the wire. And although Vitale was probably already envisioning himself in a nice pleated skirt and sports top, the Hoyas held on to win by a point. No. 16 seed East Tennessee State also came close to knocking off top-ranked Oklahoma that year, losing a 72-71 thriller, that one mercifully devoid of any talk of announcer cross-dressing.

One thing the Retrievers have to do tonight is find a way to contend with Virginia's vaunted "Pack Line" defense.

Originally designed by Virginia coach Tony Bennett's father, Dick, when he coached at Washington State, it's a sagging man-to-man that's become something of a Death Star to the rest of college basketball.

It operates on three core principles: take away the fast break. Take away dribble penetration. Take away the offensive rebound. While one defender guards the ball, the other four stay within a roughly 16-foot arc around the basket — the "pack" — to swarm anyone who drives inside and close off passing lanes.

Do all this, the theory goes, and you create hair-on-fire chaos with the other team's offense. You force them to take panicky shots from further and further away from the basket, until pretty soon it feels like they're shooting from the men's room.

Of course, the Retrievers, like every other team that faces Virginia, are sick of hearing their coaches yammer on about all this. "Oooh, the Pack Line D!" they joke among themselves. "We're so *scared!*"

Except to any sentient being who understands the game, it *is* terrifying. Virginia's defense hasn't given up more than 68 points to an opponent all season. It held Clemson to 36 points. It held Pittsburgh and Wisconsin to 37 each.

Standing near the scorer's table as his team warms up, Ryan Odom, UMBC's young, preternaturally-composed head coach, is well aware of how tough it will be for his team to score tonight.

Months ago, he and his staff had toyed with the notion of playing Virginia in an early non-conference game to kick off the 2019 season. It would be a "buy game," meaning UMBC would earn a hefty pay check for the privilege of taking a three-hour bus trip to Charlottesville to get beaten like a mule, just so the Cavaliers could pad their record and keep their fans and alumni entertained.

But the money's decent, Odom and his coaches thought at the time. *So maybe we'll do it.*

Then the next day, Virginia played Pitt – and held the Panthers to just seven points in the first half.

Seven.

Odom and his coaches watched this performance in stunned silence. When it was over, each man had the same depressing thought: *Hell, no! We're not playing them! And get embarrassed like that?*

Except now, of course, UMBC doesn't exactly have a say in the matter. You make it to the Big Dance, you play who they tell you to play.

Suddenly, an ungodly roar goes up from the crowd. The Retrievers have never played in an NBA venue. They're part of the humble America East Conference, where average attendance is around 2,000, with many in the stands staring at cell phones or making plans to get beers.

Oh, they've played non-conference games in big arenas before. But this place, the home of the Charlotte Hornets, seats 20,000 and feels mammoth. The loud noise startles them for an instant.

Looking around, they see that Virginia has just burst from the tunnel to take the court.

Oh, shit! thinks sophomore forward Arkel Lamar as the Cavaliers thunder past on their way to the opposite basket. *It's real now!*

CHAPTER 2

Why Not Us?

* * * *

Charlotte, N.C.

As the Cavaliers start their warm-ups, Lamar marvels at how big they are. He looks at their 6-foot-5 point guard, Ty Jerome, and shakes his head softly. *K.J.'s gonna guard him? Oh, man . . .*

Maura, the voluble Puerto Rican who handles the ball for the Retrievers, is listed at 5-8. Except Lamar knows that's a joke. Maura is probably closer to 5-6. He weighs maybe 132 pounds, too, making him the lightest player in college basketball. Compared to the rangy Jerome, he looks like one of the Keebler Elves.

Yet as quickly as this frisson of doubt flashes in his consciousness, Lamar dismisses it. *We're ready for this*, he thinks. *K.J. can do it. We're confident. No Monstars over there.* And anyway, didn't Bugs Bunny and Michael Jordan and their boys end up smacking those Monstar dudes around in the movie? Sure they did!

The fact the Retrievers are such a ridiculous long-shot to beat Virginia is also keeping them loose. *Everyone expects us to lose*, Lamar thinks. *So what's the big deal?* Joe Sherburne, the junior swingman, agrees. *We're playing with house money.*

We've already done what mid-major teams aim to do. Which is just to make the tournament.

To a man, the Retrievers feel their coaches have done a masterful job at preparing them for this game, getting them focused on the challenge ahead but not over-hyping the Cavaliers. And always, in every team meeting, every practice, every film session, the Retrievers have absorbed this message from Odom and his staff: you can *do* this.

You can shock the world. You can win this game.

You can make history.

Certainly, that had been the theme of their gathering at the team hotel a few hours earlier, when they had watched a killer inspirational video put together by assistant coach Bryce Crawford.

It started with a voice-over from the actor Will Smith declaring: "Being *realistic is* the most commonly-traveled road to mediocrity. You have to *believe* that something different than what has happened for the last 50 million years . . . can happen."

Backed by a pulsating techno soundtrack, what followed were clips from some of the biggest upsets in NCAA Tournament history. Four were dramatic wins by 15-seeds over 2-seeds: Middle Tennessee State knocking off Michigan State in 2016; Lehigh shocking Duke and Norfolk State beating Missouri in 2012; Coppin State, the tiny Baltimore school just a few miles from UMBC, whipping South Carolina by 13 points in 1997.

For good measure, Crawford had thrown in two of the more thrilling 14-seed wins over 3-seeds: Georgia State over Baylor in 2015 and Bucknell over Kansas in 2005.

The video ended with a silent message flashing on the screen: "AMAZING THINGS HAPPEN IN MARCH."

Finally a single word in white print remained against a tar-black background: "BELIEVE."

Oh, yes, by the time they made their way through a giddy crowd of UMBC supporters in the lobby for the short bus ride to Spectrum Center, the Retrievers were suitably fired up and focused.

Now, as the clock for the warm-up period winds down and they hoist their final shots, Joe Sherburne thinks back to something else that has helped him stay relaxed and dialed-in.

On the whiteboard in the locker room before his pregame talk, Odom had written: "Go 1-0 today."

It was the same message he'd posted before every game since the season started. But this time, Sherburne found it to be incredibly reassuring. *Coach is treating this just like any other game*, he thought. *It's a cliché, sure. But that's how we have to approach it.*

Yet when Odom finally addressed the team, the Retrievers sensed right away that something more than another rah-rah speech was coming.

Odom talked lovingly about growing up in Virginia, where his dad, Dave Odom, had been an assistant coach under Terry Holland at the storied University of Virginia for seven years. He talked about the irony of now playing a team he'd grown up idolizing – a team for whom he'd actually been a ballboy! He talked about his peripatetic journey to UMBC: a year as a lowly administrative assistant at South

Florida, then assistant coaching gigs for various durations at Furman, UNC-Asheville, American and Virginia Tech.

He talked about the lowest point in his life, when he was the interim head coach in 2015 at UNC-Charlotte — *in this very city!*—until he and his assistants were fired after the 49ers went 8-11 the rest of the season.

Then he told his players how, jobless and morose, with his family reeling because his 13-year-old son Connor was in the throes of a debilitating case of Obsessive-Compulsive Disorder, he had gloomily watched the NCAA Tournament games that year in this very building, then called Time Warner Cable Arena, wondering if he'd ever get another shot at that world, at doing what he loved to do most.

Finally, voice cracking, eyes misting, Odom thanked his players for all their hard work and the wonderful season they'd allowed him to experience. It was the first time the Retrievers had seen this kind of emotion from their but-toned-down coach.

But it came straight from the heart. They were riveted.

Ohhh-kay, Sherburne thought. *Maybe it's NOT just another game . . .*

It definitely isn't to Odom. As warm-ups continue and he paces in front of his team's bench, all he has to do is look to his left, where veteran TBS broadcasters Jim Nantz, Bill Raftery and Grant Hill, in their sharp-looking network blazers, settle in behind the microphones.

The network has trotted out its "A team," plus ace side-line reporter Tracy Wolfson, but not because it anticipates a great game for a national television audience. It's because Virginia is the top overall seed and the network sees this as a chance for Nantz & Co. to familiarize themselves with the Cavaliers. They are, after all, the odds-on favorites to be lifting the championship trophy as confetti falls from the ceiling and "One Shining Moment" blares when the tournament is all over.

At the shoot-around the day before, the TBS crew had grilled Odom at length, looking for nuggets of information and interesting anecdotes for what might be the most low-profile team in the brackets.

In fact, the only other time UMBC made the tournament was back in 2008, when the 15-seed Retrievers were whacked 66-47 by 2-seed Georgetown and its 7-2 All-American, Roy Hibbert.

When yesterday's meet-and-greet session with the announcers ended, though, Nantz had sidled up to Odom and said: "Y'know, I've been doing this for a long time. I want to be the one who calls the first 16-seed upset of a 1. Think you can do that for me?"

Maybe the long-time broadcaster says this every year to some poor wide-eyed coach bringing in his lowly team for a quick taste of March Madness before they get slaughtered and slink home.

Maybe it's just Nantz's way of breaking the ice or of trying to pump up the underdog. Odom doesn't know *what* was behind the request.

All he knows is in that moment, with Nantz studying him with that earnest expression, like a priest gazing at a penitent, Odom felt his knees suddenly go weak.

Just then, looking up in the stands, he saw K.J. Maura's father holding an enormous Fathead decal of his son and wearing a T-shirt that says: "K.J. Playmaker."

"Look up there," Odom said to Nantz. Then the coach shouted to Melvin Maura: "Turn around!"

The elder Maura did as instructed. On the back of the T-shirt, it said: 'WHY NOT US?"

Nantz nodded and grinned.

"We'll try to do it for you," Odom managed to blurt.

Was it the right thing to say? Who knows? The whole exchange caught him by surprise.

Now more than 24 hours later, when he looks over at Nantz and his partners donning headsets and studying last-minute notes and getting ready to call the game, Odom feels the butterflies doing strafing runs in his gut all over again.

Just then, the horn sounds.

There is a deafening roar from the crowd as both teams head to their benches for the pre-game introductions.

Tip-off is moments away.

As the Retrievers gather around Odom, no one is thinking about making history now.

No one is thinking about the point spread, power index ratings, the Pack D, the depressing track record of 16-seeds at the Big Dance.

Better not to think at all at this point.

Better to just go out and get after it, execute the game plan, do what the video back at the hotel said to do: BELIEVE.

K.J. Maura is right. What choice do they have?

He takes one last look around the arena and one last look at the crowd, wanting to soak it all in, to burn the image in his mind so he can summon it again 20, 30 years from now.

Man, he thinks, *look how far we've come!*

CHAPTER 3

Redemption in the Frozen North

● ● ● ●

Burlington, Vt.

UMBC's giddy run to Charlotte begins a week earlier, on Saturday, March 10, in what feels like a re-ordering of the mid-major cosmos.

Needing to win the America East Tournament to keep their season alive, the no. 2 seed Retrievers had thrashed no. 7 seed UMass-Lowell 89-77 in their first game March 3. They followed that up with a 75-60 victory over third-seeded Hartford three days later.

Next up, though, is their long-time nemesis, top-seeded Vermont, which seems to end up in the NCAA Tournament every year almost by birthright. Plus the championship game will be played in the Catamounts' claustrophobic Patrick Gymnasium (capacity 3,224), a 55-year-old facility with all the charm of a airplane hangar.

Adding to the retro feel: raffle tickets are hawked in the lobby, there's no "end-zone" seating to speak of under either basket and a folksy voice over the PA system asks: "Kids, how would you like to have your next birthday party in Catamount Country?"

Opposing teams will tell you Vermont fans are no more rude or obnoxious than the fans of other schools in the conference. Yet even as they file in before the game, many of the Catamount faithful wear a look of perpetual . . . what's the word here? . . . *irritation.*

Some say this is because it's always about five degrees outside in the Burlington winter, and many fans are senior citizens who appear to be kicking themselves for not moving to Boca Raton 10 years earlier. It doesn't help that when they finally get inside to thaw out and cheer for their beloved Catamounts, the team that helps them get through the insane New England weather, they're forced to sit in wooden bleachers that have all the comfort of galley-slave benches.

Of the preponderance of older people, Sherburne says: "I honestly did not know until recently that any students went to games. . . . The students had one tiny section behind the band. And I didn't once hear them lead a chant or anything of the sort. It's all the old folks on that front."

"And the old people trash-talk you!" senior guard Jourdan Grant marvels.

Grouchy geezers who get mouthy! To the Retrievers, the crowd is an absolute hoot and the most entertaining thing about playing in Burlington.

The visiting team's locker room here also offers its own special slice of hell.

It's tiny and musty. The hooks for the players' clothes hang over the benches, which are stuck against the walls. Which means if a player attempts to lean back to relax, he's rewarded with a sharp jab in his spinal column from a cold piece of metal.

Man, it's an uncomfortable place, Grant thinks every time he's in there. *I don't know if they do it on purpose. But you just want to get out of there . . .*

Yet all of it, the forbidding weather, the stuffy, ancient arena, the army of grumpy white-haired retirees in the stands, definitely works for the Catamounts.

They are the clear class of the conference. Since 2003, they've won the America East title five times. They've been the regular-season champs seven times.

"You can really feel it: the aura surrounding Vermont," Crawford, the UMBC assistant coach, says. "This immovable object. You'd see teams play them down the stretch and they'd just blow it."

And too often, the team blowing it has been UMBC.

As the Retrievers get ready for the 11 a.m tipoff – ESPN2 dictates that ungodly time to get the riff-raff America East championship out of the way before Power 5 action take center stage—they're fully aware they've now lost to Vermont 23 straight times.

This includes two lopsided defeats in the regular season, the latest a 28-point drubbing in early February in front of a sell-out crowd of 4,753 on hand for the debut of the sparkling new, $85 million, UMBC Event Center. ("Great opening for *that* building!" assistant coach Eric Skeeters muttered afterward.)

Yet in both losses, the Retrievers played the Catamounts well in stretches, which gives them hope here. And it's not like *this* UMBC team is responsible for all 23 losses. "Don't put that baggage on us," the players say.

There's also another issue which may or may not factor into today's game: UMBC endured an absolutely nightmarish trip just to get here in the first place.

Immediately after its win over Hartford, the weather forecast had called for an Armageddon-like snowstorm to cripple the Northeast. Afraid that flights later in the week would be cancelled, the Retrievers decided to leave for Burlington early the following morning.

The decision set off a cascading series of events that would be comical if it weren't so frustrating.

Their early-morning flight to Boston was cancelled. After five hours of sitting around the airport, they finally managed to catch a flight to Providence, R.I. Arriving there in late afternoon, they waited another two and a half hours for the team bus to arrive for the long ride to Burlington.

The snowy roads were a horror show. It was as if everyone in New England suddenly forgot how to drive and decided it would be fun to spin out into the nearest ditch. The bus crawled along at 20 mph seemingly forever. Not until 1:30 Thursday morning did they finally arrive at their hotel.

The players, though, continue to down-play the rigors of the trip. No big deal, they say. Because after all, the bus was equipped with the single most important necessity in the life of young people: phone chargers. Who even notices a blizzard when you're staring for hours at a glowing screen and texting your buddies back home?

Another fortuitous development: when the Retrievers finally arrived in Burlington, they were upgraded to a downtown hotel with a nice whirlpool and a Ben & Jerry's nearby. And in time-honored fashion, the players were able to extort from their coaches two visits to the iconic ice cream palace, with the coaches, as practically required by law, picking up the tab.

Still, even though the team managed a couple of practices at Patrick Gym, there's no telling if the long trip will have a negative effect on the players' legs – and their mental sharpness.

The Retrievers know all about Vermont's personnel. But before the game, they go through a final video session to study the Catamounts' offensive tendencies, the sets they run and how to guard them.

The coaches talk about the importance of pressing the Vermont guards without getting beat, of not allowing their bigs to get the ball where they're most effective, of guarding the three-point line.

Offensively the game plan is slightly less complicated. "Need to find ways to score baskets," Odom tells his players. "Move the ball as fast as you can."

It's what coaches have told their players since the beginning of time, or at least since the first official five-on-five was run. If nothing else, maybe all that ball movement makes the other team dizzy.

CHAPTER 4

The Work You Do in the Dark

• • • •

Burlington, Vt.

The first half is truly a schizophrenic affair.

Appearing every bit the double-digit favorite that it is, Vermont shoots 12-of-24 from the floor to take an early 30-21 lead and get the geriatric crowd howling. But UMBC finally appears to find its rhythm on offense with less than five minutes to go.

A dunk by skinny reserve forward Max Curran off a pretty pass from Jairus Lyles starts a 16-5 run. It ends with a Lyles three-pointer to pull the Retrievers to within 35-34 with just over a minute remaining, causing Vermont coach John Becker, in his seventh season with the Catamounts, to quickly call time-out.

As the final seconds of the half tick off the clock, Lyles takes a long three-pointer in front of the Vermont bench with the Catamounts' junior guard, Ernie Duncan, draped all over him. The ball swishes through the net as the buzzer sounds to make it 37-35 UMBC.

What follows next, though, is something straight out of a sit-com – or maybe the rock music parody "This is Spinal Tap."

Whooping and throwing their fists in the air, a jubilant Lyles and teammates Brandon Horvath, Arkel Lamar and Max Curran storm off the court – and promptly head to the wrong locker room.

They burst through a door and Horvath thinks: *OK, this isn't right . . .*

Like the Spinal Tap band lost backstage in Cleveland, thus begins a sheepish retreat in the opposite direction, back through the same corridor before finally linking up with the rest of the Retrievers, who are shouting "Yo, we're over here!" and chortling.

Yet as they hydrate and get serious again before gathering around their coach, there's a growing confidence that this time, the outcome with Vermont will be different.

"We can *do* this," Odom tells them. "Play like that for 20 more minutes and we go to the NCAA Tournament."

A little over five minutes into the second half, though, the Retrievers face a huge problem. K.J. Maura, the America East Defensive Player of the Year, has been guarding Trae Bell-Haynes, Vermont's smooth, high-scoring point guard and two-time conference Player of the Year.

The task has been draining. And when Bell-Haynes drives the lane between Maura and junior forward Nolan Gerrity, Maura slaps at him and picks up his fourth foul. The three-point play pushes Vermont's lead to 47-39.

Suddenly, there's a sense in the crowd that UMBC is beginning to wobble. The noise level is so loud that the old building appears to creak and shake, as if the bolts in the roof are popping out and the brick and mortar are giving way.

Odom subs Maura in and out, hoping to keep him from picking up a fifth foul. Then a decision is made: Jourdan Grant will check Bell-Haynes. Maura will guard Everett Duncan, the Catamounts sharp-shooting swingman and Ernie's brother.

Who, at 6-foot-6, towers over the elfin Maura like a giant redwood.

It's a calculated gamble, but one Odom feels he has to take. The strategy works – but not without more drama.

A lay-up by Ernie Duncan pushes the Vermont lead to 57-48 with 8:21 left, and the Catamounts look poised to pull away again.

But from that point on, UMBC looks like a completely different team. The Retrievers go on a sizzling 14-5 run. And the Catamounts suddenly can't buy a basket. They go 0-for-8 from the floor over the same period, the frustration showing on their faces.

The indomitable Lyles hits on a floater with 1:01 remaining to tie the score at 62. And now, with the final seconds ticking down and the crowd again creating an unearthly din, the Retrievers must stare down the same demons that have haunted them in the past: Vermont's vibe of invincibility, their own inconsistency at crunch time and the 0-23 losing streak.

In the end, the game comes down to two huge plays.

When Bell-Haynes drives to the basket on Vermont's next possession, his shot is blocked by Jourdan Grant and Max Curran. The ball lands awkwardly on Joe Sherburne's head. For an instant, Sherburne seems not to grasp this development.

"BALL! JOE! BALL!" the Retrievers shout as Sherburne's flails for it, terrified it's about to bounce into the hands of the Catamounts and leave him with lifelong PTSD.

But he finally gathers it in. And now 30 seconds remain as Lyles pushes the ball up-court.

Ryan Odom has no intention of calling a time-out in this situation. He doesn't want to give Vermont time to set up a defense to stop the player everyone in the gym knows is going to take UMBC's last shot.

Plus he trusts Lyles implicitly. It's a trust between coach and player that he likens to Bill Belichick's confidence in Tom Brady.

As Lyles crosses half-court with Bell-Haynes guarding him, Odom calls out a play: "EURO 2!"

Essentially it's this: Sherburne screens for Lyles. Maura gets the ball from him. Lyles finds an open spot. He gets the ball back – and hopefully puts up the game-winner.

But Lyles waves that off.

So does Maura.

They both know: the ball is already in the right hands. Why risk having something go catastrophically wrong? Like a faulty exchange between the two. Or a Vermont double-team that takes Lyles out of the play.

Yet now Odom calls another play: "CLIP!"

This calls for Lyles to set up in the middle of the court, wait for a ball screen from Sherburne and go downhill from there. *He's probably just trying to get some movement*, Lyles thinks of his coach's call. *Afraid I might get trapped.*

Uh-uh, Lyles thinks. He and Maura wave that one off, too.

What follows instead is a riveting kabuki at the top of the key, the two best players on the floor going one-on-one with everything on the line: a game, a conference title, the chance to play on college basketball's biggest stage next week.

Lyles' face betrays no emotion, but inside he's churning. Everyone on the team knows how much he wants to win this game, how it will almost kill him if he doesn't. He's still annoyed — no, check that, he's still rip-shit *pissed* — that Bell-Haynes was named Player of the Year in the conference. Again.

That should've been me this season, he thinks.

Wasn't he a beast for the Retrievers? Didn't he score 665 points as a graduate senior, the most in a single season in UMBC history? Isn't he the school's career leader in scoring average with 20.4 points per game?

Hell, yeah. But apparently it wasn't enough.

Now at the top of the key, he rocks side to side, calmly dribbling three times between his legs, readying for a shot the Retrievers have seen him work on in practice hundreds of times.

"ISO J. Lyles," they call it. Jairus isolated on a lone defender, about to break out a nasty voodoo move to make the poor guy look foolish no matter how good he thinks he is.

Bell-Haynes is playing a step or two off Lyles. The Vermont star's body language indicates he thinks Lyles will

31

drive to the basket, at least try to pick up a foul if he can't get all the way to the rim to score.

Instead, with three seconds left, Lyles suddenly rises. From 23 feet, he puts up a high-arching shot that looks pure and true from the moment it leaves his hands. *It's good*, he thinks right away.

The ball seems to hang in the air forever before it begins its downward arc and finally swishes through the net. The stands in Patrick Gym go silent. The Retrievers' bench erupts, with players leaping up and down and hugging each other.

Arkel Lamar races onto the court and tackles a jubilant Lyles. Crawford, the assistant coach who'd been standing wide-eyed in a half-crouch tracking Lyles' jumper, swoops onto the floor with his arms outstretched, as if about to take flight.

There's just one problem with all this carrying on: the game isn't over.

UMBC leads 65-62. But .06 remains on the clock.

As Vermont calls time-out and the floor is cleared, the Retrievers huddle tightly around Odom. By no means is this one in the bag. Baked into the DNA of every coach is the sense – no, the *certainty*—that disaster is always a heartbeat away.

Odom, the hoops lifer, has witnessed this phenomenon too many times to discount it.

In 2008, as an assistant on Seth Greenberg's staff at Virginia Tech, he watched in horror as a kid named Dante Jackson for Xavier hoisted a desperation shot from half-court—a complete freaking *prayer*—that banked in at the

32

buzzer to give the Musketeers a 63-62 win in OT in the Puerto Rico Tip-Off Classic.

Three years before that, Odom had seen the Hokies lose to Duke when Sean Dockery gathered in a heave from the far baseline with 1.6 seconds remaining, dribbled once and hit a wild 40-footer from just inside the half-court line for a 77-75 win that almost blew the roof off Cameron Indoor Stadium.

But Vermont has no such magic left in the building.

A long pass intended for senior forward Drew Urquhart is batted down at mid-court as the final horn sounds, and now the UMBC celebration begins in earnest.

The players mob each other in the center of the court, whooping and chest-bumping. K.J. Maura races over to Odom and screams "I told you we'd win!" He mimes shooting an arrow into the stands to where his parents sit, his dad with the Puerto Rican flag draped around his shoulders, and soon the two are hugging and weeping with joy.

Back home in Owings Mills, Md., Freeman A. Hrabowski III, UMBC's gregarious president, is also reduced to tears. A self-proclaimed "mega-nerd," the 67-year-old academic is watching this mad scene on his phone with his wife, Jacqueline. He's been Lyles' mentor for some time, and now he's in awe of the cool the young man showed in such a monstrously pressurized situation.

Stirring dimly in Hrabowski's mind for the first time, too, is another thought: how will this huge win—and especially a berth in the NCAA Tournament, with its white-hot media glare – affect the university he's lovingly headed for 26 years?

Oh, my God, we've got a great coach! he marvels. *How can we keep him?*

Maybe that's getting ahead of things. But that's how university administrators think – at least the pro-active ones like Hrabowski, whose mind seems to be churning 24 hours a day.

The raucous on-court celebration goes on for so long that an exhausted Sherburne finally wonders: *Why are we still jumping up and down?*

A two-time Academic All-American from Whitefish Bay, Wisc., Sherburne is a financial economics major with a 4.0 GPA. The last time he got less than an A in a class was his senior year in high school, when he received a B-plus in AP U.S. History.

He's often given to deep analysis of matters others don't dwell on at all. Now he wonders if there's an acceptable time-frame after which such post-game exulting becomes a cringe-worthy spectacle that has the crowd – and the national television audience – thinking: *What a bunch of dorks . . .*

Lyles finishes with 27 points, shooting 10-for-23 from the field. He's named the tournament's Most Outstanding Player for averaging 19.3 points in the Retrievers three playoff games.

"A storybook ending," Ryan Odom calls it. "So proud of these guys."

And eventually, after the awards have been passed out and the ecstatic players have sprayed each other with enough water to flood their locker room, the Retrievers are clambering aboard another bus for the trip home, still in their wet uniforms despite the Vermont chill.

They must hustle back to campus. Tomorrow is another big day, a day most of them have dreamed of being part of forever: Selection Sunday. It's the sacred ritual during which the seedings and matchups for the Big Dance are announced, when office brackets begin to take shape and teams start to dream of post-season heroics and storybook endings that still lie ahead.

With the roads mercifully clear of snow, the happy UMBC team arrives at Boston's Logan Airport, drawing quizzical looks from security personnel as they attempt to board their flight with a shiny new trophy – albeit one with the top somehow broken off in the post-game scrum – and a big sign snatched from Patrick Gym that proclaims: AMERICA EAST CHAMPIONS.

In a matter of months, a dramatic new photo will hang in the team's locker room.

It will show Jairus Lyles taking the game-winning shot against the Catamounts, seemingly soaring to the heavens, Bell-Haynes' outstretched hands in his face, the ball frozen at the top of its arc on its way to the hoop.

Underneath will be an apt inscription: "The work you do in the dark will reveal itself in the light."

CHAPTER 5

A Long Journey Validated

• • • •

Catonsville, Md.

Steve Levy, UMBC's long-time SID, is in the frozen food section of his local supermarket early the next morning when he gets a call from CBS Sports.

The network wants to do a live look-in that evening from wherever the UMBC players, coaches and fans will watch the Selection Sunday show. Can Levy help make the arrangements? Oh, and another thing. Can he arrange for Ryan Odom to get there early to do an interview with Clark Kellogg in the studio of network partner TBS, which is broadcasting the show this year?

Uh, yeah, Levy says. I can probably do that . . .

Are you kidding? Levy would get Odom and his players to juggle flaming torches astride unicycles if it meant more air time on the iconic program that for 37 years has kicked off March Madness and – cue the reverential tones of network announcers—"The Road to the Final Four."

After all, it's been 10 years since the Retrievers' lone appearance in the tournament. But now the sense of anticipation and excitement on campus is through the roof.

"This is the best time in the history of UMBC," a beaming Freeman Hrabowski tells reporters.

Although the Retrievers and their fans don't much care at the moment, the TV ratings for the Selection Sunday show have dipped in recent years. This is mainly due to a series of poor decisions by network executives that include expanding the length of the show and rolling out a clunky format that drags out the unveiling of the brackets.

Impatient viewers, after all, can put down the remote and go on-line to see the full brackets almost immediately.

Yet the show is still enormously popular with hardcore college hoops junkies. It attracts a good chunk of casual fans, too, eager to find out what all the fuss is about and why so many of their colleagues at the office Monday will be busily filling out brackets instead of doing any meaningful work.

Selection Sunday also has mass appeal because it remains the ultimate reality TV show. But unlike the contrived themes found on "Keeping Up with the Kardashians" and "Below Deck," the drama that will unfold over the next two hours isn't manufactured.

Sixty-eight teams will learn their post-season destiny. The powerhouse teams can afford to be blasé. They just want to know who they're playing, when and where. Teams on the bubble, however, must sweat it out. Are they in? Or is their season about to come to a screeching halt?

Opinions and analysis by the show's hosts are scrutinized with Talmudic rigor. Endless debate invariably follows about which teams are seeded too high and which too low, which teams lucked out and which got screwed.

Conspiracy theories abound. You haven't lived, they say, until you've turned on sports talk radio afterward and listened to the aggrieved howling and fantastical explanations callers advance for all the nefarious ways in which their team was royally hosed.

"I am constantly amazed at how much interest people have" in the show, CBS Sports chairman Sean McManus says, "specifically people who don't watch a lot of college basketball during the season.

"They will, all of a sudden, be completely captivated by the brackets."

As the 6 p.m. start time for the show approaches, the third floor Sports Zone in the UMBC Commons is filled to capacity with students, faculty, administration big-wigs and long-time supporters. The Retrievers, joined by Ryan Odom, sit at the front of the room in their gray travel sweats, facing the TV cameras and joking and fidgeting with nervous anticipation.

In the midst of it all sits a beaming Jairus Lyles, the hero of the Vermont game and the alpha male who has emerged as one of the great stories in college basketball. But Lyles' path to this exalted status was not without its challenges.

He played his high school ball at fabled DeMatha Catholic, the basketball powerhouse in nearby Hyattsville, Md. A top 100 recruit who teamed with future NBA star Victor Oladipo as a freshman, he was also a star on the elite AAU Nike EYBL Team Takeover.

Heavily-recruited by a number of major programs, he chose to play at VCU. By all accounts, this did not work out well.

Shaka Smart was the young, charismatic coach who had led the Rams to the Final Four in 2011 and with

"SHAKA-MANIA!" in full swing, the program was drawing interest from top players around the country.

VCU was especially loaded at the guard position. Lyles found himself on the bench. He played only 44 minutes and scored just 13 points all season, growing more and more discouraged. Smart could offer little encouragement that Lyles' situation would improve, so Lyles began looking around for a school where he could get playing time.

He settled on Robert Morris, the small private university in the suburbs of Pittsburgh. But this proved to be another dead-end. After only a few months, he could sense the program was not for him. He ended up leaving even before the season started.

UMBC soon beckoned. There was a scholarship available. And the school was close to his home in suburban Maryland where, he felt, he could "lock in" on both his studies and his game.

The Retrievers stunk at this point – they'd won just 34 games over the previous six seasons. Coach Aki Thomas was on the hot seat. But the opportunity at UMBC meant that after sitting out a year due to eligibility rules, Lyles had a genuine shot to show his talent, find a real basketball "home" and push toward his ultimate goal: making it in the NBA.

He arrived on campus, however, in the midst of a personal existential crisis. Striking out at two different schools, he felt, was a "wake-up call."

"I had to look in the mirror and change some things," he says now. "In college, the coaches aren't going to change for you. You gotta change for the coaches. You gotta get more mature, you gotta up your work ethic."

But putting those laudable thoughts into deeds took some time.

Lyles's debut for the Retrievers in December of 2015 was spectacular: a 27-point, 10-rebound performance against Howard. He averaged 23 points per game that first season in 2016. But it wasn't enough to keep Aki Thomas, with a dreary won-loss record of 28-95, from being fired.

Not that Lyles, Jourdan Grant and the other returning players did cartwheels that April when it was announced that a new coach was taking over the program.

"I remember talking to the team and telling them it was Ryan," athletic director Tim Hall recalls. "And I knew these kids had been thinking 'Oh, he's gonna get an assistant from Duke or someplace like that.'"

Instead, when Hall told the players their new coach was coming from a small D-2 school named Lenoir-Rhyne University in Hickory, N.C., the AD could see them deflate before his eyes. "Their body language . . . it was as if we'd gone from bad to worse."

It wasn't until the following season, Odom's first at the school, that Lyles got a true sense of the new demands that would be placed on him.

One memorable morning, he showed up at 10:58 for an 11 a.m. shoot-around prior to that night's non-conference game. Making matters worse: he was staring at his phone when he arrived on the court.

"He was practically whistling, totally nonchalant," assistant coach Eric Skeeters recalled. "And he hadn't even changed yet for practice!"

None of this escaped Odom, who quickly took his star guard aside.

"Jairus, what time is it?" the coach asked calmly.

Lyles looked down at his phone and said nothing.

"OK, well what time is shoot-around?" Ryan persisted.

Now Lyles' eyes widened. Somewhere in the recesses of his mind, alarm bells started clanging. *Hmmm, on the surface, Coach doesn't SEEM upset. So why am I getting the distinct impression that inside he's actually going ballistic . . .?*

"So," Odom continued, his voice taking on more of an edge now, "if I let you come here at 10:58 for an 11 o'clock shoot-around and you think that's OK, what are Max Curran and Arkel and K.J. going to think?

"They're going to think it's OK, too. So if *they* think it's OK, do you think we're gonna be any good this season?"

Lyles said nothing. Looking sheepish, he simply shook his head no and got dressed. Odom didn't start him that night. But he didn't cut his minutes, either. And from that point on, Lyles began to understand the focus and commitment the new coach would demand from his team.

The truth was, though, that Odom wanted even *more* from his best player. The coach wanted him to be a leader, too, a role Lyles was initially reluctant to embrace.

"Jairus was, from year one: 'I'm good, I can score the ball, you don't need to coach me like you coach the other guys,'" Skeeters said. "That was his persona. He'd come to practice, he'd practice, he'd leave. He was kind of like on his own schedule."

This detached attitude began to grate on Odom more and more.

Matters finally came to a head one day when the Retrievers were stretching in practice after a tough loss the night before. While the other players were lined up along the baseline, Lyles, as was his custom, was stretching off in a corner by himself.

"By this point, Ryan had just *had* it with Jairus not wanting to lead," Skeeters recalled. "He grabs him by the jersey and yells 'YOU GOTTA LEAD. IT'S GOTTA START WITH YOU! YOU GOTTA FUCKING LEAD THIS TEAM EVERY DAY! EVERY DAY THAT YOU DON'T LEAD, WE DON'T WIN!"

If this was Odom's version of tough love, it worked brilliantly.

From that point on, Lyles seemed to embrace his role as the Retriever's top dog. Never the peppery, rah-rah type, he began to lead chiefly by example, displaying a ferocious work ethic and commitment to winning that his teammates found inspiring.

The Retrievers won 21 games and Lyles had another terrific season, finishing second in the America East in scoring (18.9 points per game) and fourth in rebounding (6.6.) But now he had a major decision to make.

As an honor roll student who would graduate with a double major in psychology and sociology the following May, he was eligible to play another year after sitting out one as a transfer.

Should he transfer again and play as a grad student at a big-name school where he'd get more national publicity— and hence a higher profile with NBA general managers and scouts? (Georgetown, Kansas and Texas – now coached, ironically, by none other than Shaka Smart – were said to be interested.)

Or should he stay at UMBC, the school he'd grown to love over the past two years, the school where he finally felt at home?

Lyles knew all along that he planned to remain at UMBC. But he made Odom and his other coaches sweat it out. Lyles took his mom, Carol Motley, to a January meeting with Odom, ostensibly to discuss whether he should stay or leave.

Odom was understandably concerned about the possibility of losing his star guard. But he didn't pressure him to stay. Instead he counseled Lyles to talk to Freeman Hrabowski, the hugely-popular school president for the past 26 years, an educator who had made it his mission to attract bright African-American and other minority students to the sprawling Catonsville campus.

The two hit it off right away.

Lyles seemed to embrace the notion of a young university – founded in 1966—ready to show the nation that it could excel in both academics and athletics. The two talked about the importance of loyalty and values, and Lyles grilled Hrabowski on why he had remained at the low-profile school for so long.

When the talk turned to basketball, Hrabowski, the mega-geek, admitted to knowing little about the game. But he told Lyles he knew the young man was a special player. And special players could leave a lasting impact on their schools in ways they might not realize at first.

"He talked about me having a legacy," Lyles recalled. "He said I was a good basketball player and wherever I went, I was probably going to be a success. But if I stayed at UMBC, I could have a legacy that could last forever."

Lyles was immediately sold.

Soon after, he told his grateful coaches he was staying. And in the months ahead, Hrabowski would emerge as a mentor for his star player, the two meeting regularly for long talks about life, commitment and the unique pressures faced by African-American athletes on today's campuses.

CHAPTER 6

A Chance to Make History

• • • •

Catonsville, Md.

Now, sitting in this packed Sports Zone, moments away from learning who the Retrievers would face in the biggest test of their careers, Odom and his coaches can marvel at the transformation Lyles has made from remote, if supremely talented, player to approachable all-in leader over the past three years.

Immediately after Lyles' thrilling last-second game-winner against Vermont, Odom's thoughts had flashed back to an incident earlier in the season that spoke volumes about the enormous respect Lyles had earned.

The team had just come off a horrific 44-point road loss to Albany. After a grueling practice the next day, most of the players straggled back to the locker room. One player stayed behind, putting up extra shots from around the arc. That player was Jairus Lyles.

This, by no means, was an uncommon sight. Lyles was the hardest worker on the team by far and everyone knew it. But on this day, the sight of his team captain shooting all by himself made the usually placid Odom go thermonuclear.

Man, he thought, *he's the only one in here! And he's the last of my worries! He can get 20 in his sleep!*

Pulling Lyles aside, Odom asked: "Jairus, what are you doing?"

Lyles wore a puzzled look.

"Just working on my shot, Coach," he replied.

"Oh, yeah?" Odom said. "You see anything wrong here?"

Lyles said he didn't.

"You're the *only* one out here," Odom continued. "You think you can win games all by yourself? Are you a one-man team?"

When Lyles said no, Odom jerked his head in the direction of the locker room.

"Well," he said, "you need to go in there and tell the other guys, make them understand. You're a senior. This is your *one* shot at winning a championship. And you can't win it on your own. They need to be putting up extra shots, too."

Lyles nodded. This, he knew, was a responsibility he couldn't shirk. Odom had appointed him, senior Jourdan Grant and junior Joe Sherburne as tri-captains exactly for moments like this. Lyles made a bee-line for the locker room.

"He let us know what Odom said," Max Curran recalled of the incident. "It was 'If we're trying to be great, it's gotta be a full unit type of thing.' Everyone took him seriously, 'cause he shows up every day and does his job."

There were, in truth, a few eye-rolls after Lyles' exhortation. A few grumbles about having just endured a long, grueling practice. But within minutes, some eight players shuffled back on the court and joined their leader in an extra shooting session.

Sitting here now, smiling broadly and staring up at the big projection screen, surrounded by his teammates and coaches and adoring fans and waiting to see where the final chapter of his college career will play out, Lyles seems at peace with how the last few years played out.

Only one thing is bothering him. It's something he keeps trying to push to the back of his mind: earlier in the day, he'd learned that Ryan Odom had been beaten out for America East Coach of the Year by Vermont's John Becker.

Odom down-played the whole thing. He assured his star guard that life would go on, that missing out on the honor was no big deal, that those kinds of things are not what drive him. But to Lyles, this is an outrage.

He's thrilled, though, that at least the Retrievers won the league championship for their coach. And who knows what else this team can do before it's all over?

It's a little after 6 when the Selection Sunday program shows a live-stream shot of the Sports Zone and TBS host Ernie Johnson intones: "How about the UMBC Retrievers? The University of Maryland, Baltimore County! They knocked off the top seed, Vermont, on the road to make their first appearances since 2008! Wait 'til you see Jairus Lyles and K.J. Maura! That team is fun to watch!"

The room erupts in thunderous cheers, with the UMBC players beaming, leaping to their feet and high-fiving each other.

Johnson and his co-host Greg Gumbel stand at opposite ends of an enormous, futuristic-looking stage while Clark

Kellogg, Seth Davis, Kenny Smith and Charles Barkley will serve as analysts.

For the first time, there is also a studio audience in attendance numbering about 200. This will lead to a number of bizarre moments, which include Kenny Smith firing up the crowd by taking a selfie with them and Ernie Johnson joining them in scarfing down a slice of Pizza Hut pizza on live TV.

For the Retrievers, though, much of the drama bleeds from the show early.

When the first pairing for the South Regional is about to be revealed, the first school that flashes on the screen is no. 1 overall seed Virginia.

"Please not us! Please not us!" Lyles murmurs of a potential matchup. The feverish incantation is quickly picked up by several teammates.

But their pleas do no good.

"And the Cavaliers will take on no. 16 seed UMBC Friday night in Charlotte!" Johnson announces.

"Oh *shit!*" Lyles blurts. He hopes he didn't say it too loudly. A few of the other Retrievers have the same reaction.

But in the next instant, all of them leap to their feet again, whooping and shouting and high-fiving along with everyone else in the room. They're over the shock. They see it now, the Retrievers do, this tremendous opportunity they've been given.

A chance to be the first 16-seed to knock off a 1!

A chance to make history!

There is a note of bravado in their cheers, too. All over the country, one imagines, viewers are shaking their heads and thinking: *Oh, man. Poor UMBC. Got sent to Death Row early . . .*

But the Retrievers don't see it that way. *All due respect to Virginia,* their reaction seems to be saying. *But we can play with anyone in the country.*

Kellogg, though, quickly goes on to say that beating Virginia will be a high bar for any team, never mind a lowly 16-seed from a mid-major program.

"The Cavaliers are dominant defensively," he says. "And I think this is the best offensive unit Tony Bennett has ever had. I think they can go all the way to San Antonio," the site of this year's Final Four round.

In the midst of the celebration going on around him, Odom feels a number of different emotions.

For one thing, he's shocked the Retrievers didn't draw a no. 15 seed with their 24 wins and their ballsy victory over Vermont the day before. Plus he still has strong ties to Virginia. It was the school he rooted for as a kid, where his dad was an assistant coach on some of the Cavaliers greatest teams.

Even now, Odom's great friend, Orlando Vandross, is an assistant on head coach Tony Bennett's staff. Odom and Vandross were assistant coaches together at UNC-Charlotte in 2010 under Alan Major, and they've remained buddies ever since.

It'll be weird going up against Orlando, Odom thinks. And he also has tremendous respect for Bennett, considered one of the nicest guys and classiest coaches in the game.

Finally, there's another reason Odom feels conflicted. As a relatively young head coach, he is, of course, thrilled to have a team in the Big Dance for the first time. But the matchup with Virginia is daunting.

Oh my gosh! is his first reaction to the pairing. *That's like the worst! How are we gonna score a basket against them?*

Still, by the time he talks with school president Freeman Hrabowski, with the excited chatter in the room showing no signs of abating, Odom is already thinking about his game plan for the Cavaliers.

Playing them, he tells Hrabowski, "is gonna be a great experience. We're pumped. We're fired up."

Lyles has quickly come around to embrace the matchup, too. Both his parents are Virginia grads. His dad played football there before becoming a second-round pick in the 1985 NFL draft and playing six seasons for the New York Jets, Phoenix Cardinals and San Diego Chargers.

When he sees who UMBC is playing in the first round, Lester Lyles texts his son: "Maybe it's the circle of life."

Jairus hadn't thought of it that way at first. But the idea begins to grow on him.

"I don't think it's a coincidence we're playing Virginia," he soon tells reporters.

After a while, the party in the Sports Zone begins to break up. The crowd is still buzzed, though. Many, as they head for the exits, even bravely predict a colossal UMBC upset Friday in Charlotte.

Steve Levy is not quite as sanguine.

Like many in the tribe of sports information directors— the harried, over-worked, under-paid wretches responsible for providing stats and notes on their school's sports team, dealing with reporters, writing press releases, overseeing media guides and a thousand other things – he loves sports and has a boundless affection for his school.

As affable as he is, he's also a worrier by nature. And the prospect of UMBC going up against Virginia, the reigning ACC powerhouse, has him fretting even more than usual.

Well, Bennett's a classy guy, he thinks. *If they get up by 25, they won't beat us by 40 or 50. At least I hope not . . .*

CHAPTER 7

"They Don't Seem the Least Bit Nervous"

• • • •

Charlotte, N.C.

As the UMBC and Virginia players take the court for the opening tip of their South Regional game, K.J. Maura jumps up and down lightly on both feet, trying to stay loose. He looks around at the vast crowd that fills Spectrum Center, many left over from the evening's first game, a 69-59 win by no. 9 seed Kansas State over no. 8 Creighton.

It's the biggest game of his life, yet he feels surprisingly calm.

Gina is watching over me, he thinks. *She's my guardian angel.*

Maura was a toddler when Gina, his big sister, died from complications she'd had since birth. He has a tattoo on his arm that honors her: a pair of wings and a G in the middle with a halo on top.

Today, ironically, is her birthday. K.J. had prayed with his family in the hotel lobby a few hours earlier, wishing Gina a happy birthday and asking her to look out for her brother.

A win over Virginia – wouldn't that be an epic birthday present for his sis?

Many of the Retrievers fans that have made the drive down from Catonsville are not feeling nearly as serene as Maura, however. Exhibit A is Freeman Hrabowski. UMBC's leader is sitting in the lower seats across from the Retrievers' bench with his wife Jackie. Next to them is Greg Simmons, the school's vice-president for Institutional Advancement.

Simmons' role is to serve as a human Valium for his excitable boss. Even as the Cavaliers win the opening tip and the game begins, Hrabowski seems on the verge of hyper-ventilating. If he gets too worked up, Simmons is empowered to intervene, theoretically with everything from deep-breathing exercises to calm-inducing mantras to actual physical restraint.

Both teams get off to a ragged start, possibly owing to the late start time. The second time Virginia has the ball, Joe Sherburne is matched up against the Cavaliers' senior forward, Isaiah Wilkins.

Wilkins is the 6-foot-8 stepson of NBA Hall of Famer Dominique Wilkins, who was nicknamed "The Human Highlight Film" for his above-the-rim game and his arsenal of swooping, soaring throw-downs.

The younger Wilkins, while playing a more grounded game than his famous step-dad, can ball, too. He's the ACC's Defensive Player of the Year and the key component of the Cavs' smothering Pack Line defense.

When the ball is dumped inside to Wilkins on this sequence, Sherburne leans on him aggressively. It feels as if he's pushing against a steel girder.

But surprisingly – at least to Sherburne—Wilkins doesn't try to bulldoze his way to the hoop. Instead, he dribbles twice, turns, and puts up a wild hook shot that misses.

A good omen, Sherburne thinks. *He backed down.*

But not everyone sees it as an encouraging sign for UMBC. When Wilkins scores the game's first basket seconds later on a little turn-around one-hander in the lane, TBS analyst Seth Davis tweets two words: "Virginia. Sharpie."

It's only 2-0 Cavaliers. But to his hundreds of thousands of Twitter followers, Davis is effectively saying: *This one's over. Write Virginia in your bracket. In ink.*

It's a familiar Seth Davis schtick, writing off a team way too early. And as usual, it stirs things up in the Twitterverse. It makes the fans of whatever team he's dissing positively apoplectic. Which is the same effect it's having now on Zach Seidel, UMBC's 27-year-old director of digital media, who is sitting near courtside, staring at the words on his laptop and quickly going Chernobyl.

C'mon, he thinks, *it's been 10 years of bad basketball! But we're good now! At least give us 'til halftime!*

As the game goes on, Seidel launches into a hilarious series of clapbacks that delights his Twitter followers:

"Seth, it's 5-3 us."

"Virginia leads UMBC 7-6 with 11:58 remaining, someone please inform Seth."

"We are winning, 9-6, Seth."

Followers of @UMBCAthletics are equally enthralled by the digs Seidel takes at other doubters weighing in, those convinced the Retrievers will be run out of the gym at any moment. ("We won 24 games and a conference title, it's not like we are a YMCA team, dude," he answers one cynic.)

All of it, it turns out, is vintage Seidel, a funny, good-humored dude who can nevertheless quickly get the red ass at even the mildest disrespect directed at his school.

He's steeped in all things UMBC. He graduated from the school in 2012 with a degree in media communications and got a master's in human-centered computing three years later. His parents both went to UMBC and his sister, Kara, is a senior there.

He's worked a number of jobs in sports communication for the university. But when they made him director of digital media, they discovered they had a natural on their hands. They had someone with a deft, humorous touch for promoting the school on social media, but someone who could also gently smack down the trolls when it was called for.

The best Twitter accounts, Seidel feels, are ones that have personality. Don't just spew out play-by-play, is his philosophy. *Jairus Lyles hit a jumper from the corner. UMBC leads by two.* Please. Put up too many of those and the next sound you hear --- ZZZZZ—will be three-quarters of your followers dozing off.

Instead: answer people! Crack jokes! Have fun! It's all about interaction. Yet Seidel takes great pains not to be mean-spirited, but rather self-effacing, when he posts about other schools and engages with their followers.

Maybe, he says, you can't be this witty and light-hearted doing social media for, say Alabama football, where every

Saturday is treated like a shooting war and head coach Nick Saban keeps the entire program on Defcon 1 footing.

But mid-major programs? Heck, at least make the posts *entertaining*. And Seidel is good at this. So good that soon another admiring Twitter denizen is moved to write: "Whoever is running the @UMBCAthletics account tonight is doing the Lord's work."

Both teams have trouble scoring early – the Retrievers go over five minutes without a basket during one stretch. But they're playing excellent defense to stay with the Cavaliers, who, as usual, work their offense with maddening patience and milk the shot clock for all its worth.

Arkel Lamar hits a three to give UMBC the lead for the first time, 9-7, with 11:06 left in the half. And after Sherburne hits a three-pointer from the corner to cut the Virginia lead to 16-13 five minutes later, analyst Bill Raftery notes that UMBC doesn't seem to be "the least bit nervous."

Raftery is right. Actually, instead of being anxious, the Retrievers are playing with a fair amount of swagger.

With 4:32 remaining, Maura's long three from the side of the key ties the game at 16-all. He launches into his trademark celebration, miming cocking a bow and firing an arrow into the crowd, which has some of the blue-blood Virginia fans tsk-tsking at the effrontery.

And at the media timeout, with the UMBC fans roaring and on their feet, broadcaster Jim Nantz seems caught up in the moment.

"Some might be saying," he exclaims, "'U might be Cinderella!'"

When the Virginia defense fails to rotate, Lyles gets a rare clean look at the basket and hits a long three to put UMBC up 19-16 with 3:06 left. Of the Retrievers last six baskets, five have been threes, giving them hope that their early shooting woes are over.

Yet the last two minutes of the half are a flurry of drives to the basket, with each team seemingly determined to assert its physical presence and head into the intermission with the lead.

Virginia's senior guard Nigel Johnson slithers through the lane for a layup to tie the game at 19 with 1:58 left. Arkel Lamar scores on a tough one-hander high off the backboard to give the Retrieves a two-point lead, but Ty Jerome hits a lean-in jumper in the paint that ties the game at 21-21 with 54 seconds left.

When Lyles' desperation heave at the buzzer clangs off the back rim and the two teams head for the locker room with the game still tied, Nantz cries: "People all over saying 'What's going on in Charlotte?!'"

No one seems quite sure.

But this much is clear: mighty Virginia is being handled so far.

Yes, a full 20 minutes remain in the game. And the Cavaliers are a poised and talented team coached by one of the best in the business. If their Pack Line D holds and their grind-it-out offense can start wearing down UMBC, the odds are they prevail.

Nevertheless, there's a palpable stirring in Spectrum Center, a sense that this no. 16 seed shows no signs of backing down and that something special might be unfolding here before the night is through.

The rest of the country is starting to take notice, too. Zach Seidel discovers this moments later when he stares at his TweetDeck with a puzzled frown and calls out to Steve Levy, his boss.

"Steve," Seidel says, "UMBC's internet, the main site, crashed."

A TweetDeck is a social media dashboard that helps manage Twitter accounts. Seidel's lets him keep track of his own personal column, the @UMBCAthletics account and Twitter posts across all of UMBC's sports.

Except now, the screen on his TweetDeck has gone black. He turns to the person on his left, who happens to be Jess Ramberg, the America East's social media head.

"Is this normal?" he asks.

Ramberg says no. She looks over at his screen. Suddenly the tweets start scrolling so fast they're a blur.

"That's weird," Ramberg says. "I don't know what's going on."

What's going is this: the sheer volume of digital traffic coming UMBC's way is overwhelming its site. Seidel's cell phone is buzzing with every notification possible. Across the entire country, college basketball fans are tuning in to the drama taking place in Charlotte, where a school most have never heard of tries to pull off the impossible.

CHAPTER 8

We Can Steal This One

. . . .

Charlotte, N.C.

In the UMBC locker room at halftime, there is excited chatter and hand-slapping, but also the knowledge that a lot more work lies ahead.

The mood feels just right to Ryan Odom. No silliness, but no tension, either. There is a certain emotional alchemy coaches like to see from their teams at the intermission. In this case, there's no question the confidence level of the Retrievers has grown exponentially.

In particular, they're feeling good about their defense. They haven't shot the ball well – only 35 per cent from the floor. They've also committed some dumb turnovers. But their energy level is impressive.

They're making Virginia work hard at both ends of the court—perhaps harder than it's worked all year.

The close score and the relentless pressure being put on the Cavaliers causes UMBC's assistant coach Nate Dixon to muse on one of his favorite theories about athletic competition: the puckering of a certain bodily orifice in times of great stress.

Of the Cavaliers, he thinks: *We knew going in that they don't blow teams out. It's just their style of play. It's not that they're not good enough. So if you can keep it close . . . We always joke, if you keep it close, your butt-hole gets a little tight. So that was our whole idea. We're not supposed to win. They're supposed to win.*

Dixon was Ryan Odom's associate head coach at Lenoir-Rhyne and worked alongside him as an assistant at UNC-Charlotte. He's been with some big programs, notably Florida, where he was an assistant to college basketball's newest young savant, Billy Donovan, from 2003-2005.

Dixon coached such future NBA players as David Lee, Cory Brewer, Al Horford and Joakim Noah. He's seen how even the game's best stars can choke – or at least grow smaller—under pressure, allowing anxiety to unsettle them as they try harder and harder to perform better.

Now he's just watched the Cavaliers shoot 39.1 per cent from the floor in the first 20 minutes. From three-point range they were an abysmal 11.1 per cent. If the mighty no. 1 overall seed keeps clanging shots at this rate, Dixon figures, you won't need a proctologist to see whose butts are tightening.

One person seemingly unworried about this fabled anal phenomenon is Odom, who exudes the same calm now that he always does.

In the lost years before he took over in 2016 and led UMBC to a 21-13 record, the Retrievers had endured eight straight losing seasons under former head coaches Aki Thomas and Randy Monroe. They'd won just 56 games in that span.

The musty Retriever Activities Center, known as the RAC and first opened in 1973, could be a dreary place on game nights, with sparse crowds and students staying away in droves. Now the youthful-looking Odom is being celebrated for the team's dramatic turn-around and the new pride and excitement it's brought to the UMBC campus.

In a way, though, it's ironic he's even in this business at all. He grew up as a famous coach's son; his dad, Dave Odom, was a successful head coach at East Carolina, Wake Forest and South Carolina from 1979 to 2008, winning 406 games.

But when Ryan was young, Dave Odom would be away for months at a time, between coaching, recruiting and working Five Star camps in the summer. Even though Ryan loved the perks of being a coach's son, he wasn't sure that kind of peripatetic life was for him.

He was a star point guard at D-3 Hampden-Sydney College in Virginia and as a senior economics major, did an internship on the trading floor at Bank of America corporate headquarters in Charlotte. Although he enjoyed it, he quickly decided banking wasn't in his future, either.

Seeing his older brother Lane doing well as a graduate assistant for Wimp Sanderson's Alabama program made him take another look at coaching. And after getting caught up in the excitement of seeing Dave Odom's Wake Forest teams win back-to-back ACC championships in 1995 and 1996, Ryan decided he might give the family business a shot after all.

But few outside the UMBC basketball program know of the incredible stress and upheaval Odom and his wife, Lucia, have dealt with in their home life.

Over the years, their oldest son, 13-year-old Connor, has suffered from a crippling case of Obsessive Compulsive

Disorder. OCD is characterized by unwanted thoughts and fears (obsessions) that lead to repetitive behaviors (compulsions) that significantly interfere with day-to-day life.

In Connor's case, an overwhelming worry about germs compelled him to wash his hands over and over until they were chapped or even bleeding. He also began taking hours-long showers in an effort to feel clean.

One alarming shower ritual had his fevered brain mandating that he pump the soap dispenser exactly four times and only wash with the fifth dollop. If he messed up the count, he had to start all over again. If towels were crumpled on the floor, he would touch one and say: "Oh, I didn't touch that one right" and feel the need to touch it again.

His battles with anxiety traced back to second or third grade, when a boy in his class would often throw up for unknown reasons. Soon Connor was obsessed about getting sick and vomiting.

By the summer of 2015, though, the OCD was consuming his life. He couldn't go to school. He wouldn't let anyone touch him, not even Lucia. The Odoms couldn't have visitors in their home.

Desperate for answers, the Odoms had Connor seen by a succession of medical experts, including pediatricians, therapists, psychologists and psychiatrists. He had brain scans. None of it helped much. He was prescribed anti-anxiety meds, which also did little. Connor continued spiraling downward at an accelerating pace.

Adding to the enormous strain on the family, Ryan, then the interim head coach at UNC-Charlotte, was fired along with his entire staff. Before the firing, knowing Ryan had been in charge of a program for the first time and focused on his high-pressure job, Lucia had tried not to worry him with the more disturbing details of Connor's behavior.

But now that he was home every day, Ryan could see that Connor was getting sicker.

"It was the worst point in our lives with everything going on," Lucia said.

In audio and video recordings she made of Connor standing at the bathroom sink or taking a shower, the boy's anguish is visceral.

"I can't do anything!" he cries at one point as he brushes his teeth. When his dad, off-camera, says soothingly "Yes, you can," the answer is a swift "*I CAN'T!*"

"It's like I'm being tortured!" he moans in the shower. "It's like I'm in jail! It's like my mind is shackled! And I don't have the key to get the shackles off! Dear God, please help me to get out of the shower and stop having these terrible thoughts!"

Ironically, the only thing that could lure Connor outside was basketball — the family vocation.

It's probably one of the germier things you can do, he realized. But somehow the rhythmic bouncing of the ball against the patio stones in his back yard or the hardwood floor of a gym, along with the exhilaration of putting up a shot and watching it sail high through the air before swishing through the net, relaxed him.

Basketball, he felt, was not there to judge him, the way a lot of people did. It helped clear his head.

But eventually, even that ceased to be an escape. At a national AAU tournament, he spent three hours in the shower and missed the game. He was distraught, at his lowest point.

"The hardest thing I think I've ever dealt with in my life is knowing I couldn't fix my son," Lucia told ESPN's "E:60" program for a segment on Connor's disorder.

Then came a glimmer of hope.

As Lucia and Ryan searched everywhere for a way to help their son, she came upon a book in her local library titled "Saving Sammy." Written by a woman named Beth Alison Maloney, it detailed how the author discovered her own son's OCD was caused by a previously unknown strep infection.

For Lucia Odom, it was a revelation.

This is what's wrong with Connor! she thought.

No, Connor wasn't having sore throats. He had no other symptoms of strep, either. No fever, no swollen tonsils or lymph nodes. Nevertheless, when the Odoms had him tested for the bacterial infection, his numbers were sky-high.

This led to a diagnosis of Pediatric Autoimmune Neuropsychiatric Disorder Associated with Streptococcus, or PANDAS.

"In all honesty, it wasn't a weight off my shoulders," Connor would say later. "It kind of made me feel worse. 'Wow, there *is* something wrong with me.'"

He was prescribed antibiotics to combat the strep. His OCD improved, but not enough to constitute significant progress.

His therapists felt he needed more intensive help. So that summer, Lucia and Connor moved to Nashville, where the boy began treatment at Rogers Behavioral Health, a specialized mental health care facility.

Lucia rented a nearby corporate apartment sight unseen. This, predictably unsettled Connor. Suddenly there was a scary new germ-filled environment to navigate and fear.

The new living arrangements stressed everyone in the family. By this point, Ryan had taken over as head coach at Lenoir-Rhyne and was living near the school in Hickory, N.C.

Owen, the Odom's youngest son, remained at the family's home in Charlotte, cared for on a rotating basis by Ryan's parents and Lucia's mom. Lucia, meanwhile, was trying to run her own business, a clothing boutique that required her to travel frequently to buy merchandise.

Connor stayed for three months at Rogers and responded well to a treatment called Exposure Response Therapy.

The therapists drew up a hierarchy of his fears – being hugged, shaking someone's hand, having his mom touch him, etc. He was asked to rate each on a scale of 1 through 7, with 7 essentially being "Provokes high anxiety, impossible to do" and 1 being "I can do that pretty easily."

The idea was to focus on each fear, let the accompanying anxiety reach its peak and endure it until it starts to subside. This cycle of exposure, anxiety and subsequent relief is timed and repeated at each level on up the scale. As the patient gets used to, or habituated, to his or her fears (obsessions), the need to rely on compulsions to deal with them wanes.

The therapy was mentally exhausting. Yet when he finally went home, Connor pronounced himself as "80 to 85 per cent" better.

In April of the following year, Ryan Odom was named head coach at UMBC. The move to Maryland was jarring for the whole family, coming so soon after they had finally reunited in Charlotte. Connor, enrolled in a new school, St. Mary's in Annapolis, where he hoped to play basketball, had a particularly tough transition.

Slowly at first, and then with increasing rapidity, his OCD came back. Embarrassed, he didn't initially tell his parents. But soon the raging fear of germs and the endless hand-washing and showers had returned with a full fury.

By August of 2017, he was back at Rogers Behavioral and Lucia was fighting with the family's insurance company, which was balking at paying the $1200 per day for his treatment. When he returned home, he felt better—not as well as after his first trip to Nashville, but determined to get on with his life and not let the disorder consume him.

So here he is, not long removed from a second round of therapy, a happy-looking 16-year-old sitting in the stands at Spectrum Center with the rest of the raucous UMBC fans, waiting for the second half to start.

His father is thrilled to have him here.

In the midst of the team's exhilarating season, Connor's issues and his growing distress have consumed everyone in the family. Ryan's laser focus on his team gives him temporary relief from worrying about his son— the shrinks call it "compartmentalizing."

But Connor's OCD is never far from his thoughts.

"No matter what's going on in your professional life, good or bad, you're always concerned with family," Ryan tells people.

Yet now, as the Retrievers prepare to take the court for the second half, he's as dialed-in as ever. His team has played with verve and passion. The moment – and the stage – has not proven too big. So his message now is simple.

"We just gotta go out there and do what we did the first half, only a little better," he says. "And our run's gonna come. We need to stay in the game with our defense. We can't take a play off.

"And then offensively," he continues, "when we have opportunities to go in transition, we want to go. And if you feel a shot early in transition, take it. But we don't want to take bad shots, either."

Before heading out to the tunnel, the Retrievers gather in the middle of the room, clasp hands and shout: "1-2-3 Together!"

Reading their body language and seeing a quiet resolve in their eyes, Odom and his assistant coaches have the same thought: *Keep the score close and we can steal this one.*

A little butt-tightening on the Cavaliers part might help, too.

CHAPTER 9

Shock in the Building

• • • •

Charlotte, N.C.

Joe Sherburne wastes no time in getting the Retrievers off to a strong start in the second half, quickly delivering another metaphorical punch in the mouth to Virginia.

The junior forward drives the lane in the opening seconds for a scooping, and-1 layup and makes the free throw for a 24-21 UMBC lead.

He's just rumbled his way to the basket with the brawny Isaiah Wilkins draped all over him. But since it's become *de rigueur* during UMBC's heady post-season run to attach the word "cerebral" to any mention of Sherburne, the TNT announcers again focus on his intellect as opposed to his athleticism.

"First basketball player in America East history ever to make Academic All-American first team," Jim Nantz tells the viewers. "He's never made a B in his life. Which I can relate to. Then again, I never made an A."

"I never made a B!" Raftery chimes in as the stand-up routine continues.

Certainly, Sherburne is a brainiac by any measure of the word. But he can also ball, as he's proven over and over since he took up the game as a kid. He's a strong shooter – seventh on the school's all-time scoring list – and rebounder, as well as a steadying presence on the court when the game gets tight.

His quirkiness and dry, sardonic sense of humor are a constant source of amusement for the Retrievers, even though his best lines often seem to float over their heads. After high school, he prepped for a year at Brewster Academy, a tony New Hampshire boarding school, where some of his teammates would go on to play for UConn, Louisville, Washington and Arizona.

The high-level competition improved his game markedly. But UMBC was the only D-1 program to make him an offer, which he accepted in part because of its – cue the requisite oddball alert—*mascot*.

"I had never heard of (the school) and then I looked at the mascot and I thought, 'OK, if worse comes to worse, I'll come here because they have a dog mascot, and it'll be fine," he told The Baltimore Sun.

He's also a huge fan of the "Harry Potter" books and movies. He's read the seventh installment, "Harry Potter and the Deathly Hallows," three times. Cementing his off-beat cred: family members have heard him reciting whole passages of Potter movie dialogue in front of the bathroom mirror.

Now, though, the free-spirit side of him is nowhere to be seen. His face is a picture of grim concentration. The Retrievers understand the need to get off to a fast start; none have embraced this notion more than their erudite forward with the altar-boy looks.

After an air-ball by Kyle Guy, K.J. Maura races the ball up court and feeds Sherburne with a pretty behind-the-back dump-off pass. Sherburne swishes a jump shot from four feet beyond the arc, and just like that it's 27-21.

If you believe in foreshadowing, what happens next does not portend well for Virginia.

Sherburne, a huge Green Bay Packers fan, backpedals down the court and does the "Discount Double Check" celebration move of Aaron Rodgers, the one where the quarterback mimes showing off his championship belt in his State Farm commercials.

The UMBC bench erupts in a joyous frenzy of the goofy arm-swinging and leg-kicking dance from Fortnite, the team's favorite video game. And after Kyle Guy bricks a free throw and K.J. Maura scampers untouched down the lane for a layup, Tony Bennett promptly calls time-out.

It's 29-22 UMBC. There are still over 17 minutes to play. But Bennett's normally placid features betray genuine concern.

The Cavaliers look clueless. Equally puzzling, they seem lifeless.

The Retrievers, on the other hand, struggle to control their growing excitement as they huddle around Ryan Odom. Every facet of their game is clicking perfectly. But they know this one is far from over. They have to keep their focus.

You know they can come back in a heartbeat, Sherburne thinks. *They're not the no. 1 team in the country for no reason.*

Coming out of the time-out, the Cavaliers seem to have decided on a new tactic. Maybe they need to take more advantage of their size, muscle up on the smaller Retrievers, go to more of a power game.

Maybe they can pick on the shortest player on the court, the one who, even with the goatee and wisp of a mustache, still looks like he's headed to a middle school dance after this is over.

So it is that the next time Virginia has the ball, Jerome goes to work, posting up on the right block. He gets the entry pass and starts backing Maura down, dribbling with his left hand and extending his right elbow—bumping, bumping, bumping the little guy—before spinning and putting up a soft one-hander off the glass.

Seeing this, Retrievers assistant coach Eric Skeeters curses softly. *If they figured that out,* he thinks, *we're done! They're gonna do this the rest of the half!*

The Virginia bench erupts and Bennett gives a barely-perceptible nod of satisfaction. But any hope that this is the start of a turn-around for his team is short-lived. Lyles and Sherburne quickly bury back-to-back 3's and just like that, the UMBC lead has ballooned to 35-24.

It's the biggest margin Virginia has trailed by all season. The crowd noise is deafening now. It seems as if the whole building has thrown its allegiance to UMBC, sensing that something special might be happening.

UMBC's pep band is rocking, playing with a ferocious intensity. And Senior Cara Jaye, who plays True Grit, the school's mascot, is nodding and bopping on the end line near the cheerleaders while trying not to pass out.

Jaye is 23, from Olney, Md. She graduated from UMBC two years earlier as a music major, but her love for performing as a mascot keeps her coming back. She loves both the anonymity of the job and the challenge of bringing the character to life.

But when she woke up a day earlier, she was sick, necessitating a frantic run to CVS for cold medicine. Now she's woozy from the meds, over-heated from being encased in an all-fur costume and close to hyperventilating from the excitement of seeing her beloved team play with such swagger.

The rest of Retriever Nation is equally enthralled by what it's seeing.

In the stands, surrounded by whooping and high-fiving students and alumni, Freeman Hrabowski is so emotional he's close to tears. He was scheduled to speak at a research conference in California today, but gave the keynote address a day early so he could fly across the country to be with his basketball team.

Now his cell phone is blowing up with text after text from fellow academics in Berkeley. They're supposed to be listening to another STEM speech about now. But instead they're watching the game and sending messages to Hrabowski, all with variations of "Freeman, this might happen!"

"There's some shock in the building, no doubt!" Nantz exclaims.

As the game continues, it's obvious that the Cavaliers are getting rattled.

With Maura nipping at his knees, Jerome puts up an air ball from beyond the right block. On the next trip down the court, Virginia's normally-steady floor leader throws the ball away passing to senior guard Devon Hall, who is breaking the other way.

As Jerome and Hall exchange looks of frustration and Tony Bennett rolls his eyes and shakes his head, two things have become clear.

First, the Pack Line defense is not intimidating UMBC. The smothering double-teams that have rattled so many of their opponents are failing to materialize. The Cavs are getting beat in transition. And the Retrievers are getting open for perimeter shots and knocking them down.

Secondly, the tempo of the game is not favoring Virginia. While most teams that are heavy underdogs and out-manned talent-wise attempt to slow the game down, sometimes to a listless slog, UMBC is speeding up the pace.

It feels right to the Retrievers, who are playing fast and loose, like they're on a playground somewhere, or on one of those magical runs in practice when everything feels right and every shot seems to go in.

For the Cavaliers, though, the tempo appears to be frantic and unsettling. They seem out of sync offensively.

Passes are arriving a hair too late, players are cutting to the basket a step too slow, shooters are not squaring up completely before they let the ball fly.

Hard as it is to believe, things are about to get even worse for them.

Much, much worse.

CHAPTER 10

Echoes of Chaminade

* * * *

Charlotte, N.C.

During a practice earlier in the week, the Retrievers had done a drive-and-kick drill that − put charitably—did not go well.

The drill was called Ball Ahead 3. Player A would drive into the paint and pass the ball out to Player B. Assistant coaches Bryce Crawford and Eric Skeeters would converge on Player B with their hands up, elbows literally in the driver's face. The drill was designed to simulate the incredibly small window UMBC would have to get a shot off against Virginia.

On that day, the window looked more like a porthole. Not only could no one make a shot, they were also missing ugly. Balls would clang off the front of the rim. Or smack off the side. Or thud against the backboard like a cantaloupe hitting a brick wall.

Or they were air balls. In a real game, of course, an air ball is that most humiliating of all outcomes, the one that sets off a predictable wave of derisive chants and hoots from the other team's fans.

But even in practice they can be unnerving. Damaging to a shooter's psyche.

Oh, my God! thought Crawford. *We're in trouble!*

Crawford, 28, is in his second year at UMBC. He was on Ryan Odom's staff at Lenoir-Rhyne and came to Catonsville with him. Crawford is young enough to relate to the lifestyles and sensibilities of the players and is beloved for the energy and positivity he brings to every game and practice.

But as the Retrievers did the drive-and-kick drill over and over again, his face clouded over.

Nothing changed. It was like watching a hoops version of "Groundhog Day." The Retrievers were trapped in a time loop of hideous shooting. It felt like they'd missed 100 shots in a row.

We're gonna get pounded! Crawford thought. And he wasn't the only member of the coaching staff who was concerned.

Yet now, if there's any residual psychological damage left over from that dispiriting drill, UMBC is hiding it well.

Up by 14 with 15 minutes left, no one on the floor seems the least bit hesitant of jacking up a shot – from *any-where*—if he can get a step on a defender, shake him for an instant. And no one exemplifies this growing confidence more than Jairus Lyles.

In fact, the hero of the last-second win over Vermont and the team's go-to scorer all season long, is about to put on a show.

It starts when he comes off a Dan Akin ball-screen at the top of the key, gets the slightest separation from Virginia's Devon Hall, and quickly puts up a jumper from five feet beyond the three-point line.

Hall lunges desperately to block it but instead lands awkwardly on Lyles' feet, sending the Retrievers' star reeling backward.

The shot lands with a *clonk* in the crevice between the rim and backboard. But Hall is whistled for the foul. Ignoring the jeering chorus of Virginia fans, Lyles calmly sinks all three foul shots for a 38-24 UMBC lead.

"It's Virginia's biggest hole of the whole season!" Nantz informs viewers.

After a three-point play by Jerome – an off-balance layup over Akin and a made free throw – cuts the lead to 11, Hall slips and turns the ball over. UMBC rushes it up-court and Maura finds Lyles with a pretty pass on the right side of the key.

Lyles gathers the ball in mid-stride, sets himself and lets it fly, burying a three-pointer over 6-foot-10 Jack Salt to make it 41-27 with 14:57 left. He shoots a baleful glance at Salt as the UMBC fans erupt and the decibel level in the arena reaches ear-bleed level.

More than any other shot UMBC has hit thus far, this one feels like a dagger.

It sends an unmistakable message to the Cavaliers. What Jourdan Grant sees on their faces now is this: *Wow, these guys are coming at us!*

It's the first time all season that Virginia has faced this kind of relentless, tidal-wave of offensive pressure. And judging by the puzzled expressions of Salt and his teammates, they're not quite sure how to deal with it.

This is hardly the first time that the UMBC players have seen Lyles, their team leader, carry the scoring load.

But they're clearly energized by his swagger. In the stands, Lester Lyles, who played in plenty of pressure situations throughout his football career, marvels at how easy his son is making the game look.

"I've never seen him play that way!" the elder Lyles will tell reporters later. " . . . I think he rises to the occasion."

Bryce Crawford sees the way UMBC is attacking Virginia – racing up and down the court, eagerly putting up bombs from anywhere—as a direct reflection of how Ryan Odom teaches the game.

He empowers guys to shoot the ball, Crawford thinks. *He will yank your behind out of the game if you're not shooting the shots we practice every day. That's why we can turn it on and play like this.*

With each body-blow Virginia absorbs, their fans in Spectrum Center grow more and more quiet. Their apprehension is almost palpable.

Sure, there's plenty of time left. And this is a veteran team that, while clearly off its game now, is unlikely to lose its composure and is coached by one of the best in the business. The thinking – at least among the die-hard Virginia faithful—seems to be: *Hit a few shots, get a few stops . . . heck, we're right back in this.*

Yet for the older fans, the ones steeped in the history of this proud university and its basketball teams, an awful thought is worming into their consciousness: *Chaminade.*

On the night of Dec. 23, 1982, tiny Chaminade, then an NAIA school, dumbfounded the country by beating the no. 1 ranked Cavaliers and their 7-foot-4 All-American center, Ralph Sampson, in a pre-season game in Honolulu.

The Silverswords' 77-72 win is still considered by many to be the biggest upset in college basketball history. Sampson was the most dominant big man in the game, a two-time NCAA player of the year who would go on to win the award for the third time the following spring. (UCLA's Bill Walton was the only other three-time winner.)

A Catholic school with an enrollment of some 850 students, Chaminade was the unlikeliest of giant-slayers. Its setting, despite being not far from world-famous Waikiki Beach, was decidedly humble: it shared a campus with a local high school.

Its coach, Merv Lopes, was paid such a paltry salary ($10,000) that he also worked as a guidance counselor at a local high school. According to a 2007 interview with Sports Illustrated, Lopes begged towels for his players from local hotels, drove the team bus (an old Navy surplus van) and washed the players' uniforms himself in the athletic department offices, "which had been a boiler room when the campus served as a military hospital during World War II."

Virginia, by contrast, was the toast of the college game. The team was 8-0 and had just been paid $50,000 – more than double Chaminade's annual basketball budget – to play in Hawaii after a pre-season tournament in Japan.

The "stop-over game" on the way home was supposed to be a breeze for the Cavaliers. Despite it still being early in the season, Virginia had already been sorely tested by two of the best teams in the country.

The Cavs had just played what was called "The Game of the Decade" against Georgetown and its' All-America center, Patrick Ewing, in which Sampson scored 23 points, hauled in 16 rebounds and blocked seven shots in a 73-62 win.

In Japan, they had beaten a Houston team led by Akeem Olajuwon and Clyde Drexler – the leaders of the vaunted Phi Slamma Jamma—despite Sampson sitting out the game with an intestinal virus.

The Silverswords, on the other hand, had just come off a loss to Wayland Baptist University, another small school in Plainview Texas. Moreover, in two previous matchups against Virginia, the 'Swords had been crushed both times.

Their big man, sophomore center Tony Randolph, who had played against Sampson in high school, stood just 6-foot-6. The rest of the roster consisted of a rag-tag bunch of oddballs and free spirits with enough holes in their games to be over-looked by most D-1 programs

"The guys came from all different backgrounds and weren't too stable," Lopes, their coach, told SI, as if describing a mental ward. "But they played hard and played together."

They also had a unique way of preparing to face Sampson, Lopes divulged to the magazine. It involved their 5-foot trainer standing on a chair and holding up a broom to simulate the towering presence they'd be facing.

And on that fateful December evening, with a crowd of 3,300 looking on, Chaminade did what all big underdogs try to do: they kept the game close and stole it at the end.

Randolph played out of his mind, scoring 19 points on 9-for-12 shooting and holding the great Sampson to 12 points. Clinging to a two-point lead in the final seconds, the

Silverswords were the beneficiaries of a controversial call on Virginia's Othell Wilson for carrying the ball. And they made three free throws at the end to seal the five-point win as the jubilant crowd rushed the court.

Although Chaminade would begin hosting the big-name Maui Invitational the following season, the game against Virginia wasn't even televised. Also, only a few newspaper reporters were on hand. So not until Christmas Eve had already dawned on the East Coast did word start to filter out about the Silverswords' incredible feat.

In Hawaii, newspapers trumpeted the headline: "Yes, Virginia, there is a Chaminade." At the time, Chaminade had been considering changing its name to the University of Honolulu, which sounded, at least to administrators, like a more impressive name for an institution of higher learning.

But the renown that came with knocking off the Cavaliers soon convinced school fathers that the name Chaminade was perfectly fine. Why, suddenly it even sounded Harvard-esque! A place where any aspiring student willing to work hard could receive an education on a par with any of the top-notch schools in the country!

In much of the mainland U.S., initial reports of the upset were considered so preposterous that news organizations, including a brash new all-sports outfit called ESPN, refused to run them without confirmation.

Ironically, as UMBC's second-half domination of Virginia continues, one person in Spectrum Center *not* thinking of that amazing long-ago upset is Dave Odom, Ryan's Odom's dad.

But back in '82, he was a first-year assistant coach on Terry Holland's Virginia staff when the decision was made to have an idyllic stopover in the middle of the Pacific for some sun, fun and Silversword-bashing.

Odom emerged from that loss as shocked as everyone else in Virginia's traveling party.

"We had the best team in the country by far," he told people. "We had the best player in college basketball and great players around him. And we had the best coach . . . in Terry Holland."

For years, what Dave Odom remembered most was something Holland told him at the Honolulu airport the next morning, as the team readied for the long flight home.

"David," Holland said, "what happened last night was so unbelievable, so surreal, that by the time the news gets back to the East Coast . . . nobody will believe it. And then they'll go on to something else."

Holland was wrong, of course. The UVA-Chaminade game has remained a topic of fascination in basketball circles ever since that fateful evening in 1982. It has also haunted Cavaliers fans for years. It's haunting some of them here in Charlotte, 36 years later.

Yet as Dave Odom sits in the stands now with his wife, Lynn, watching his son coach in the biggest game of his life, that long-ago defeat in Hawaii is far from his thoughts.

That's because a shocking new upset could be developing in front of him right now. And he knows if UMBC can hang on and beat Virginia, this one would be unbelievable, too.

And every bit as surreal.

CHAPTER 11

"Can This Be the Night?!"

● ● ● ●

Charlotte, N.C.

Jairus Lyles continues to put on an otherworldly performance.

With under 13 minutes to go, he comes off a Joe Sherburne ball screen and drives the left side of the key. Kyle Guy gets caught in the traffic jam. And when none of the other Cavaliers rotate over to help, Guy watches forlornly as Lyles cruises to the rim for an unmolested layup and a 43-29 UMBC lead.

Virginia, meanwhile, has gone stone-cold.

When Devon Hall's open jumper caroms off the back of the rim seconds later, it marks the 10th straight miss from three-point range by the Cavaliers. For the game, they're now an ugly 1-for-11.

Virginia knows it's in trouble. This is a smart and incredibly-talented team. Yet it's devoid of anyone who can take a defender off the dribble and create his own shots. Now that they're down by 14 and their outside shots aren't falling, the Cavs seem to be flailing.

The TBS cameras linger on Tony Bennett gazing out at the court with a thousand-yard stare.

"They're just not the same personality we've watched all year long," Bill Raftery says of the Cavaliers. "It's tough when you're the coach and you just don't recognize your team."

So much of that, though, has to do with the brilliant performance of Lyles, who is slicing and dicing the Pack Line defense at will.

After Ty Jerome's 12-foot jumper rims out, Lyles brings the ball down-court, knifes through the lane and switches the ball from his right to left hand in mid-air for a flashy layup and a 16-point UMBC lead.

Bennett has seen enough. He looks like a man who's just eaten a bad piece of fish.

Virginia quickly calls time-out.

A visibly-hyped Lyles exhorts the UMBC fans to get on their feet and get loud. There are two odd things about this request. No. 1, the fans are already on their feet. And no. 2, if it gets any louder, the building will start to levitate.

"Can this be the night?!" Nantz exclaims over the tumult. "The shocker of all shockers in the history of the tournament?!"

When play resumes and a Wilkins tip-in pulls Virginia within 14, TBS sideline reporter Tracy Wolfson, who has been reporting from behind the Virginia bench, delivers this observation:

"Tony Bennett was really calm in the huddle. But you can definitely sense the shock. He said 'We are in a tight game right now and in order to get out of it, we need to get some stops.'"

But this appears to be wishful thinking. The Retrievers are in full attack mode now, their belief in themselves growing by the minute.

The next time UMBC has the ball, Lyles drives into the paint and puts up an off-balance floater to give the Retrievers a 47-31 lead with 10:23 left.

"The kid's on fire!" Nantz shouts!

"He is! Raftery agrees. "He *believes!*"

As Lyles trots back on defense, he glances over his shoulder as Hall inbounds the ball to Guy. The two Virginia guards seem dazed, both shaking their heads softly as if rouse themselves from a bad dream.

You can see it on their faces, Lyles thinks. *They're shocked. They're frustrated. They don't know what to do.*

Lyles has scored the last 12 UMBC points, and he's not through yet.

With a little over seven minutes to play, he finds a seam in the Virginia defense on the left side, drives the middle and puts up a spinning layup to keep the UMBC lead at 15.

It's at this point, though, that UMBC comes face to face with a problem that, while not totally unexpected, has the potential to be catastrophic: their floor leader is beginning to cramp up.

His calf muscles are screaming. His toes feel like they're burning.

The long season is definitely taking its toll. He's been playing 38 minutes a game for weeks. And now, in addition to carrying the scoring load for the Retrievers, he's guarding Kyle Guy, the Cavaliers' sharp-shooter and All-ACC first-team selection, who seems in perpetual motion.

All game long, Virginia has been running Guy off three and four and five screens to free him for a shot, with Lyles doggedly chasing after him and banging off the big bodies in his way.

Lyles leaves the game, bent over and hobbling. UMBC trainer Brandon Gehret tears open a packet of Gatorlytes, the powdered mixture designed to replace heavy electrolyte loss. He mixes it with eight ounces of Gatorade and gives it to Lyles.

Lyles takes a sip and recoils. To say the stuff tastes horrible is an understatement. There is pond sludge that's more palatable.

But Lyle swills it and checks right back into the game. Seemingly OK, he gashes the Virginia defense once more and puts up a floater that bounces high off the rim before finally dropping through the net.

But Gehret, watching the stiff way the Retrievers' captain shuffles back on defense, senses his work is not over.

Sure enough, moments later, with UMBC up by 14, Lyles' legs seize up again. He heads to the sideline and sprawls on the floor at the end of the bench in obvious pain. This time he waves away another offering of Gatorlytes. *Are you kidding me, bro?*

Gehret's next suggestion doesn't go over any better. He wants Lyles to drink a concoction of apple cider and vinegar.

Athletic trainers have sworn by the reviving properties of this mixture for years. Knock back a mouthful, they say, and muscle cramps instantly disappear. However, it, too, does not go down easily. To some, it makes Gatorlytes taste like a fine Bordeaux.

Lyles gets a whiff of the stuff, makes a face and declares flatly: "I'm not drinking that shit."

At this point, UMBC's team physician, Matthew Sedgley, says: "He needs salt!" With that, the good doctor runs back to the media tent. When he returns, it's with another tried-and-true home remedy for dehydration that athletes have known about for years: peanut butter crackers.

And so it is that with less than five minutes left in the game, a national TV audience, as well as anyone in Spectrum Center looking up at the Jumbotron, is treated to the sight of UMBC's luminescent guard furiously licking the salt crystals from an orange-colored cracker.

(As seemingly nothing in sports is more important than product placement these days, word of this quickly reaches the Charlotte corporate headquarters of Lance Snacks, makers of the crackers Lyles is serially slurping.

(Within minutes, an enterprising PR type there tweets out a screen grab of the moment to preserve for posterity — and possibly for future ad campaigns as well.)

Ryan Odom, meanwhile, appears unconcerned that Lyles is in pain, with muscle spasms rippling up and down his legs and his toes locking up. Not for a second does Odom think his best player is done for the night.

The guy is too tough to call it quits, Odom thinks. Has too much heart. Not to mention too much emotional capital invested in this game, too.

Instead Odom calmly says to Lyles: "When you're ready, just go back up."

Meaning to the scorer's table. To check back in.

What UMBC's coach *is* concerned about, however, is what a desperate Virginia team is likely to do next.

Down by this much late in the game, the Cavaliers are going to tear up their playbook, he tells the Retrievers.

"There will be no more working the ball around," he says. "No more running the clock down. Their better players" — he's thinking Guy, Jerome and Wilkins — "are going to start going to the basket. And we're going to have to deal with that.

"On defense, they're gonna start trying to trap us," he continues. "They're gonna come after you, try to rake the ball. You gotta take care of the ball, go meet passes. But you gotta maintain spacing.

"And if they come at you, I don't want you to be tentative. Play forward. Take what they give you. Make them pay if they come after you."

In the back of his mind, Odom knows he has the perfect weapon to counter any furious trapping the Cavaliers attempt.

The perfect weapon stands all of 5-foot-6 and weighs 132 pounds.

But he plays much, much bigger than that. And he can definitely make Virginia pay.

CHAPTER 12

The Facilitator Takes Over

* * * *

Charlotte, N.C.

If Jairus Lyles has delivered one punishing blow after another to the Cavaliers, it's K.J. Maura who seems intent on throwing the figurative uppercut that finally drops them to the canvas.

The diminutive guard is UMBC's Energizer Bunny. Teammates and coaches have marveled for years over his incredible conditioning. Even after a grueling practice that leaves the rest of the Retrievers gassed and ready to puke, Maura is practically whistling as he heads to the showers.

Couple this with his amazing ball-handling and court savvy, and trying to trap him is like trying to trap fog.

Of all the certified underdogs on this team, Maura has perhaps the most compelling story.

He began playing basketball in his native San Juan, Puerto Rico at age 5, at the urging of his father Melvin. But it wasn't until he started watching the NBA that he fell in love with the game. His heroes were the so-called "little guys": Steve Nash, Carlos Arroyo, Jason Kidd and John Stockton.

All were at least 6-foot-1 or taller, though, which meant they towered over K.J. But that was OK. Maybe he was delusional, but the realization he was short wouldn't hit him until years later, when people began insisting he'd never play at a higher level because of his size.

He proved the doubters wrong by playing at a private high school called St. Francis, which had some of the best sports teams on the island. But the basketball roster was stocked with talented players.

"We had like 15 guys who could play at any level," he recalled, including some with Division I potential. Which meant Maura spent a lot of time on the bench.

He was invited to a youth national team camp, but the message he received from the coaches – *You're too short, kid, try baseball*—was similarly discouraging.

In his junior year, frustrated and depressed, he went to a camp run by the Miami Tropics. This was a high-level amateur team whose founder, Art "Pilin" Alvarez, helped a lot of Boricua youngsters raise their profile and get college scholarships.

"We start scrimmaging, he's out there with something like 100 kids," Alvarez told ncaa.com of seeing Maura for the first time. ""You watched him play – he's so pesky and he's so small, but you can't steal the ball away from him.

"And I just went 'Wow.' We have guys who are 6-foot-4, 6-foot-5, 6-foot-8, the whole bit. But that whole week, he was the one who continued to impress me."

One of the island kids Alvarez had helped was J.J. Barea, who stood just 5-foot-9 and went on to play for Northeastern University and the Dallas Mavericks. Inspired by this and similar success stories, Maura played well at a big tournament in Vegas later in the week.

That performance caught the eye of Rex Morgan, the varsity coach at Arlington Country Day School in Jacksonville, which had one of the most celebrated prep programs in the country.

That first year at ACD, Maura recalled, opposing players "looked at me like I was barbecued chicken." A former assistant coach, Patrice Days, described him as "iPhone thin" back then.

But Maura quickly proved himself defensively, relentlessly guarding taller opponents a full 90 feet down the court and making them expend so much energy that they'd become exhausted and careless with the ball.

In a holiday tournament in 2012 against Huntington Prep, the West Virginia powerhouse ranked no. 1 in the country, he founded himself checking Andrew Wiggins after a defensive switch. The 6-foot-7 Wiggins was the nation's top-rated player and would go on to play at Kansas before being selected no. 1 overall in the NBA draft by the Cleveland Cavaliers.

He was also a full-blown celebrity in that part of the country.

As both teams warmed up before the game, Maura had noticed Wiggins sitting at a table court-side signing autographs, with hundreds of people waiting in line for his signature. *Wow, this guy is really a big deal!* Maura thought. It fired him up even more to be playing against such high-level talent.

Wiggins tried posting Maura up and quickly picked up a pair of offensive fouls before ending up on the bench, scowling and frustrated.

The highly-touted prospect went on to finish with 21 points and 11 rebounds in the Huntington win. But Maura had made a statement: he was fearless enough, and crafty enough, to guard players far taller than him.

With his speed and quick feet, he was a terror for anyone bringing the ball upcourt, able to anticipate spin moves, make steals and – no small feat—get in the other guy's head, too. He went on to average in double figures for both points and assists and ACD won a state championship his senior year.

Proving the naysayers wrong once more, he landed a scholarship at D-1 Abilene Christian. But a shoulder injury ended his season early, and a purge of the coaches coupled with a failed drug test had Maura on the move again.

His next stop was College of Central Florida, where he was named to the junior college All-America team and led the country in assists with 9.6 per game.

Now he was getting calls from programs like Iona, Towson and Utah State.

"I was starting to think I belonged," he said.

But the JUCO game can be a jungle. Players often tend to be a lot more selfish. Everyone's trying to get looks from D-1 coaches—and eventually scholarships—so the emphasis on personal stats is palpable.

Maura, on the other hand, saw himself as a facilitator.

Instead of trying to score 30 like everyone else, what made him successful was finding his teammates in transition and getting everyone involved in the offense. That's what he did best. And that was what coaches wanted from him, too.

Only Towson University in Baltimore County ended up offering a scholarship. But when Maura couldn't visit the school because he was scheduled to play in the JUCO All-Star Game in Las Vegas, the Tigers signed another point guard.

The message was clear: Maura's services were no longer needed there.

To the rescue came Ryan Odom, who had just been introduced as the new coach at UMBC. Selling a little-known program that had gone 4-26 and 7-25 the two previous seasons was a tall order, but Odom was up to the task.

He told Maura that his no. 1 priority was to establish a winning culture in the program, and eliminate the losing mind-set that might have infected any of its players. Then he said the magic words that won Maura over for good: "I know you're a winner. So we need you."

"The school gave me the love I needed," Maura would go on to tell everyone.

The Retrievers definitely need their lightning-quick point guard here at Spectrum Center, with under five minutes to play, Lyles cramping and out of the game, and Virginia pressing all over the court.

Taking an inbounds pass from Sherburne, Maura blows past Guy and gets the ball over the half-court line. He dribbles out of a trap set by Guy and Devon Hall, drives the lane and finds Sherburne on one wing for a wide open three-point shot.

Sherburne's jumper misses, but the contrast between Maura and the Virginia guards in the closing minutes couldn't be more obvious.

Maura zips around the court fearlessly – even *joyfully* – eluding double-teams, firing pinpoint passes to his teammates and looking around at the big crowd, seemingly drinking in the moment.

Kyle Guy and Ty Jerome, on the other hand, look ashen-faced and exhausted. At the under-four-minute timeout, sideline reporter Tracy Wolfson sees no fire in the Virginia huddle.

They look defeated, she thinks. *They have no answers. They don't know how to get back in it.*

Seemingly fortified by his intense burst of cracker-licking, Lyles checks back in to cheers from the UMBC fans. With 3:58 left, he drives into the paint and puts up a floater to put the Retrievers up by 14 again. Yet he's soon grimacing and jogging stiffly back on defense, prompting Bill Rafferty to shout: "He's hurt again! Except when he gets the ball!"

Seconds later, Maura steals a pass by Kyle Guy and now it's Nantz who yells: "What has happened to Virginia?!" And when Lyles finds Arkel Lamar on the baseline for a wide open three and a 61-44 UMBC lead, the arena devolves into pure bedlam.

As he backpedals on defense, Lamar shakes his head and wags his tongue, an homage to his childhood hero, the great Michael Jordan. The UMBC fans are on their feet and screaming to the heavens, joined, it seems, by most of the crowd. On the Retrievers' bench, another exuberant round of Fortnite dancing breaks out.

A sense of inevitability is quickly taking hold. But Odom and his staff, while thrilled with how the game is going, are not ready to celebrate just yet.

Etched in Bryce Crawford's mind is a wild 2013 game from the Atlantic 10 Conference Tournament at the Barclays Center in Brooklyn, when Charlotte pulled off a ridiculous 68-63 win over Richmond despite being down by three points with 4.7 seconds left.

"Craziest finish I've ever seen in my life," Crawford is fond of telling people.

The bizarre ending was highlighted by Richmond coach Chris Mooney going nuts after a foul call on one of his players. Ripping off his jacket, he stomped toward the refs like he was packing a shiv and about to use it.

For this performance, which hearkened back to the full-on-psycho days of Bobby Knight at Indiana, Mooney quickly earned two technical fouls and an ejection. The crowd at Barclays was small that day – the game had started at noon and this was the very first time the conference tournament was played there. Nevertheless, the fans that were there gave the distraught Mooney a standing ovation for his unhinged performance.

In the midst of all the histrionics, Charlotte guard Pierria Henry ended up shooting 11 straight free throws to seal the win for the 49ers. Henry was lucky his arm didn't fall off from fatigue.

In post-game remarks to reporters, he said it felt as if he'd been on the foul line for a half-hour.

Is anything like that Hindenburg ending in Brooklyn likely to happen to UMBC with just a few minutes remaining?

No. But these are coaches. Their mindset is: disaster lurks everywhere. Doubt and uncertainty is baked into their DNA.

And the sun is only 50-50 to come up tomorrow.

CHAPTER 13

"Put Some Respeck On It!"

• • • •

Charlotte, N.C.

Virginia calls time out after the Lamar three. But there's little Tony Bennett can do at this point.

There's nothing he can say to his team to stop the beating it's taking. This is UMBC's night and the drawn faces on the Cavaliers as they shuffle over to listen to their coach suggest they've known that for some time.

It's like the soul got taken out of them, Max Curran thinks.

Maura is brilliant over the game's final minutes. He skitters and scoots around the court, indefatigable as always, coolly breaking the Virginia press and quarterbacking the half-court offense. When he sinks a pair of free throws to push UMBC's lead to 65-48, the TV cameras capture his dad, Melvin, proudly waving the giant Fathead of his son.

"It's just amazing!" Nantz proclaims of the improbable scenario unfolding before him. "I've never seen anything like it!"

Seconds later, trapped in a corner with two defenders on him, Maura makes a heady two-handed jump-pass that finds Arkel Lamar all alone on the left baseline for an easy dunk and a 67-48 UMBC lead.

Everybody knows the game is over. But with no slaughter rule in college basketball – the subject was last kicked around, with varying degrees of seriousness, when Tulsa beat Prairie View by 91 points in 1995—the Cavaliers continue slogging up and down the court.

Yet in their hollow eyes and slumped shoulders, there is no pretense that they can launch some grand comeback for the ages. *They don't even want to take the ball out!* Maura thinks. And when Jourdan Grant takes a nifty feed from Lyles and hits a three from the corner to expand the Retrievers' lead to 72-52 with 1:10 to go, Nantz finally casts aside the innate caution every broadcaster feels about declaring a game over too early.

"A 20-point lead!" he cries. "And the greatest upset in the history of this tournament is going to happen!"

Only now does Ryan Odom turn to Nate Dixon on the bench to casually ask: "Hey, did you do anything on Kansas State? We have anything on them?"

But the scouting report on the Retrievers' next opponent will have to wait. When Joe Sherburne sneaks down the lane and takes a pass from Grant for an uncontested layup and the exclamation point on this 74-54 rout, the celebrating by the UMBC players and their fans officially kicks into high gear.

As the last few seconds tick off the clock, the TBS cameras linger on Odom.

As always, he appears composed. The barest hint of a smile plays on his lips. But then comes a moment when he shakes his head and silently mouths a single word that seems at once profound and totally appropriate for what has just taken place: "Wow."

"Shock and awe in college basketball!" Nantz declaims.

When the final horn sounds, the jubilant Retrievers spill onto the court, whooping and hugging and breaking out their signature—and epically-bad—Fortnite dance moves. Assistant coach Bryce Crawford spreads his arms and again appears to fly onto the court, this time in a Superman-like pose that will be captured on the cover of Sports Illustrated.

Moments earlier, a beaming Maura had run over to Odom and bellowed: "I told you so!" It was a reprise of his Joe Namath moment a week earlier, when he had guaranteed an improbable victory over Vermont. Now he follows this up by shooting imaginary arrows of love up in the stands at his mother and father, where Melvin still clutches his son's Fathead and a partially-unfurled Puerto Rican flag.

Lyles, who finishes with 28 points on 9-for-11 shooting – with 23 of those points coming in the second half—rushes over to the UMBC section and starts smacking palms and shaking hands like he's running for governor.

On the Virginia bench, the anguish is profound.

Forward Mamadi Diakite, who had earlier furiously clapped his hands and exhorted his teammates to "Wake up! Wake up!" stares vacantly at the celebrating Retrievers. Isaiah Wilkins is red-eyed and inconsolable.

Many of the other Cavaliers look down at the floor, some with their hands over their heads as if trying to blot out the memory of what just happened. Their disconsolate fans – some openly weeping—head quietly for the exits.

After the rest of the Retrievers leave the floor to bois-
terous cheers, Lyles, Maura and Jourdan Grant join Ryan
Odom on the court for a post-game interview with Tracy
Wolfson.

In her 14 years with CBS Sports, Wolfson has covered
everything from NCAA men's basketball championships
to Super Bowls to U.S. Open tennis to SEC football. But
viewers have rarely seen her as animated as she is right now.

"You guys made history tonight!" she begins. "Never
before had a 16 beaten a 1! And you did it in dominating
fashion! How did you get it done today?"

"We just believed in each other, man!" Lyles says. "We
came in with the mindset of believing in each other and
competing. And that's what we did. We got the W."

Standing quietly off to one side, Odom wears a soft
smile, obviously delighting in the joy he sees on his players' faces as they talk to Wolfson. It would be totally out of
character for the modest, reserved Odom to be jumping
up and down at a moment like this, or to be bubbly with
excitement.

Odom does not do bubbly. Or anything that even comes
close. He's as chill as they come with the media, after both
wins and losses.

Still, for a coach whose team has just done the impossible and is suddenly the toast of college basketball, he seems
amazingly composed as he talks about his players, about
how proud he is of them and how much credit they deserve
for their incredible performance.

Only when Wolfson brings up Dave Odom, who has
been in the stands watching his son coach for the past two

hours while having a quiet nervous breakdown, does Ryan Odom's smile widen.

"I'm sure he's a proud papa," he says. Then jokingly: "And I'm sure when we get home, he'll tell me everything I did wrong."

When Jairus Lyles finally leaves the court – the last Retriever to do so – he spots a familiar figure striding toward him. It's Freeman Hrabowski, grinning happily and seemingly recovered from the psychic stress that consumed him for most of the game.

The two men embrace, the university's biggest cheerleader and his protégé, the basketball star whose transcendent play over the past two weeks has been a thing of beauty to witness.

"So proud of you!" Hrabowski says. "God is so good!"

Fittingly, it's Zach Seidel, UMBCs nimble digital wiz, who comes up with the perfect social media posting for this amazing night.

Taking to his TweetDeck, Seidel announces triumphantly, complete with intentionally-hip misspelling: "PUT SOME RESPECK ON IT! WE HAVE DEFEATED NO. 1 OVERALL SEED VIRGINIA 74-54!"

As everyone who witnessed this game knows, everyone filing out of Spectrum Center into the darkened streets of Charlotte and everyone watching at home, history lurched in a different direction tonight.

They said 16-seeds were 0-135 against 1-seeds? And that the Retrievers were almost two-touchdown underdogs to upset one of the best college basketball teams ever? All of that, the odds and the stats that said it couldn't be done, toss them in the fireplace, drizzle them with lighter fluid and burn them.

This is officially the maddest March Madness ever.

And for UMBC, the school the whole world seems to be Googling, the madness is just beginning.

CHAPTER 14

"What Do We Do Now?!"

• • • •

Catonsville, Md.

Some 435 miles to the north, on the darkened campus of UMBC, it's spring break.

At even a good-sized, modern-looking school, this can be a particularly bleak affair. Classroom buildings and parking lots are deserted. Dormitories are mostly empty. There might as well be tumbleweeds blowing around, like you see in the old Westerns.

When the sun sets, it's crickets—both actual and metaphorical.

Yet just before midnight, when the Retrievers' thumping of Virginia is official, the few students still here throw down their remotes and rush outside into the cool March air, whooping and cheering.

They're joined by a well-oiled contingent of other students just returned from watching the game at nearby bars. Maybe a dozen others – this group fortified only by Buffalo wings and the contents of various veggie, cheese and cookie platters – join them from a watch party at The Commons, the student activities center.

All are eager to celebrate this upset for the ages, this incredible whipping of the mighty Cavaliers. But to say they're new at this sort of thing is a vast understatement.

What results is an awkward milling-about of almost comical proportions.

As he watches the euphoric scene around him — people hugging and weeping with joy, tearing off T-shirts and flinging caps in the air—freshman bio major Mike Spano thinks: *This is the greatest night of my life!*

Just a few hours ago, though, Spano was peeved. It seemed as if every mention of the Retrievers, on both TV and social media, had been negative. All the so-called experts had written them off. Virginia was going to stomp them, crush them, bury them — that was the consensus opinion.

Then, to add insult to injury, came the Seth Davis Sharpie insult! Before anyone on the court had even broken a sweat!

Spano took it all personally, growing more and more irritated.

It was like UMBC was worthless! he thinks. *Like we were nothing! But now, all around me, is this . . . this explosion of happiness!*

Yet Spano also senses two possible stumbling blocks that he and his fellow celebrants will have to overcome in order for this celebration and this epic outpouring of Retriever Nation pride to continue:

No one has a clue what to do next.

Or where to go.

A lone reporter for The Baltimore Sun, working on a reaction piece for the next day's newspaper, talks to a junior named Patrick Ogoh. Ogoh attempts to explain why, unlike on other campuses where a once-in-a-lifetime athletic feat might be commemorated with mass beer-soaked gatherings, bonfires, impromptu parades and even — if things get out of hand—the occasional torching of a police cruiser, he and his fellow undergrads seem unsure as to exactly how to cut loose.

"No one gave UMBC a chance," he says. "We're known as the brainiacs of Maryland. We don't even have a football team. Now we won? This is incredible!"

Yet Ogoh is also amused at how many of his fellow geniuses seem blissfully unaware that the Retrievers' singular win occurred in merely the first round of a tournament, and that a tough second round opponent awaits them Sunday night.

They're yelling "We did it!" and "We won!" Like we won the national championship, he thinks.

Not far from campus, Ronny Meghairouni, a senior at Catonsville High scheduled to attend UMBC in the fall, has been watching the game in the basement of his parents' house with a couple of friends. Due to cable issues, the three are huddled around a laptop, taking in a grainy version of the action instead of catching a clearer version on a high-def TV.

For days, Meghairouni has been telling his buddies that the Retrievers would beat Virginia. And not only *beat* the Cavaliers, but go all the way to the championship game. Naturally, they thought he was insane.

Yet as the game against Virginia goes on and UMBC's lead gets larger and larger, his friends eye him with both awe and suspicion, wondering that kind of dark mojo he has working for him that he remains so confident.

When the final horn sounds at Spectrum Center, all three friends start screaming. The noise is loud enough to be heard in Wyoming, never mind on the third floor of Ronny's house, where his parents are sleeping.

Within seconds, his mother, Eptissam Mawardi and his father, Issa Meghairouni, are bounding down the stairs to see what horrible calamity has befallen their son and his pals.

The family is from Syria – Ronny was born there. And in that war-torn country, such screaming could signal anything from an exuberant wedding celebration to a tenant discovering his apartment building leveled by an artillery shelling.

Relieved to see the commotion is caused by something as mundane as a basketball game, Eptissam and Issa quickly join in the revelry, beaming as Ronny cries over and over: "THIS IS MY SCHOOL!"

Some 30 minutes later, roughly half the revelers gathered near The Commons have made their way to the bronze statue of True Grit, the Chesapeake Bay Retriever and school mascot. Here, in the shadow of the RAC, the Retriever Activities Center where UMBC played it's basketball games before moving into its glittering new arena, there is more celebrating and carrying on.

Smiling students take selfies with True Grit, caress his ample rump, kiss his cold snout and slosh beer on his ears as they jostle for position in group photos. A few of the more rambunctious and beered-up revelers tip over trash cans and toss chairs in a nearby courtyard.

Yet when they're reprimanded by an older man – "Hey, party all you want! But don't throw things!" – they actually apologize and disperse peacefully. A witness to the scene, UMBC economics professor Nick Kelly, who is there with his wife Laura and his golden retriever Keeper, marvels at the respectful exchange.

These might be the most polite and joyful drunks he's ever seen. *Not exactly sofas on fire when the Terps* won, Kelly thinks.

The reference is to a tradition at the state's flagship school, the University of Maryland, a 30-minutes drive south on I-95. There, the student body has been known to celebrate big basketball wins – and even losses - by burning couches along Route 1 in College Park, toppling light poles and ripping street signs out of the ground.

After a memorable 83-81 victory over Duke in 2016, Terps fans commemorated the occasion by attempting to set a storefront on fire, lighting toilet paper and throwing it into the crowd, waving flares, climbing rooftops and taunting police with chants of: "Bring in the horses!"

That night, helpfully attempting to explain the chaotic scene to reporters, one Maryland student said: "No. 1, fuck Duke. No. 2, we're the best team in the country. No. 3, we're the best at rioting."

Mercifully, there is none of that menace and out-of-control vibe around True Grit. Instead, Kelly thinks, the trash can tippers and chair-tossers simply got caught up in a we're-so-shocked-we-won, we-don't-know-what-to-do moment.

Kelly himself is here, he says, because tonight's win was the greatest upset moment of his life. And because his belief in superstition – already fairly strong—has grown exponentially in the past week.

The dictionary defines superstition as "a widely held but unjustified belief in supernatural causation leading to certain consequences of an action or event, or a practice based on such a belief."

As Kelly will tell you, yeah, that's pretty much spot on for him.

On the Saturday that the Retrievers upset Vermont to win the America East title and punch their ticket to March Madness, the 38-year-old academic had watched the game from his home in Elkridge, Md.

With two minutes left, he had tweeted the host of a local sports-radio show to say: "If we win, I'm kissing the dog." Everyone knew what he meant. And when Jairus Lyles' game-winning three ripped through the net at the buzzer and caused a packed house in snowy Burlington to go silent, an elated Kelly jumped in his car, made the five-minute ride to campus and kept his promise.

He's here now because as the Retrievers widened their lead over Virginia, as the pounding of the Cavaliers became more brutal and the inevitable UMBC win came more and more into focus, Kelly realized there was something he *had* to do to keep the team's mojo going.

With the plaza around True Grit's statue nearly deserted, he hands his cell phone to a stranger and says: "Mind taking a picture?"

The stranger obliges, waits until everyone's ready and pushes the button. And the image he captures belongs on a Hallmark card.

There are Nick and Laura bending down and kissing the damp, scruffy nose of the bronze retriever, looking as if they're about to crack up at any moment. And there is Keeper, staring intently into the camera, a green bandana decorated with tiny shamrocks tied around his neck.

It is, after all, the wee hours of St. Patrick's Day.

CHAPTER 15

University of a Million Brackets Crushed

• • • •

Charlotte, N.C.

After going through the handshake line with the dejected Virginia players and their coaches, the Retrievers sprint to their locker room, their joyful bellowing echoing off the corridor walls.

Inside, they launch into a jangled, off-key version of "One Shining Moment." This is the schmaltzy anthem about hard work, perseverance and making the most of opportunities that plays as the winning team cuts down the nets after the tournament's championship game.

But the Retrievers version quickly dies out. In fact, it dies out after the very first line − *The ball is tipped* …—due to a problem that is at once embarrassing and thoroughly predictable: no one knows the rest of the words.

Well, *one* player does: Joe Sherburne. He memorized them from the old March Madness video games from 2005 and never forgot them. He knows the rest of the stanza goes like this:

And there you are
You're running for your life,

You're a shooting star.

But what is he going to do, belt out the lyrics all by himself? That would be awkward. Maybe even beyond weird.

Instead, the Retrievers start a new chant, "NO MORE PERFECT BRACKETS!" relishing the agony they have just caused everyone whose chances of winning the office pool went down the toilet.

Amid the bedlam, players check their cell phones, which are blowing up with congratulatory texts, tweets and emails from all over the country. When Joe Sherburne pulls his phone from his pants pocket and sees all the messages, his only reply is a quick tweet that says: "WTF!?"

Instantly this strikes him as somewhat lame. He wishes he could summon something more clever and incisive. But like everyone else in the room, he's still in a state of shock. *If I knew we were gonna win*, he thinks, *I would have had something planned out . . .*

The collective astonishment at UMBC's good fortune is not limited to the players, either.

When Nate Dixon, Bryce Crawford, Eric Skeeters and Griff Aldrich, UMBC's director of recruiting and program development, gather in a small area reserved for coaches, each man looks at the others in dazed silence.

Finally it's Aldrich—hands clasped upon his head in the classic body-language of the befuddled—who gives voice to the thought on everyone's mind: "What the *hell* just happened?"

On social media, it's as if the whole world is discovering UMBC and basking in the glow of its stunning accomplishment. The school once derided as "U Made a Bad Choice" and "University of Maryland Back-Up College" is now the "University of a Million Brackets Crushed," as its Twitter feed proclaims.

It's also the no. 1 topic trending on the social networking service world-wide. And reaction is pouring in from everywhere.

Dan Rather, the legendary CBS newsman, tweets: "Do they make glass slippers this big? UMBC carved their program on the Mt. Rushmore of Cinderella stories. I've never seen this much shock and awe on the hardwood. I watched every minute.

"Whenever you hear, 'we can't,' tell them UMBC."

Meanwhile, Steph Curry is talking up the team on Instagram. The Golden State Warriors All-Star guard has posted a photo of the triumphant Retrievers swarming the court after the final horn with the caption: "Every Dog has their day! Congrats."

Another NBA great, Baltimore native Carmelo Anthony, texts his congratulations to Eric Skeeters, who promptly shows it around to the whole team. And Joe Sherburne, the Wisconsin native, hits up Aaron Rodgers on Twitter, sending along a clip of the Retrievers' forward hitting that early second-half three and reprising the star QB's patented "Discount Double-Check" move.

(Rodgers will get back to him the next day, tweeting "I see you Joe." To which Sherburne, utterly agog that his hero has actually deigned to respond, lets out a yelp and musters only this in reply: "I'll send you some gear.")

Even the Fortnite creators get caught up in UMBC's norm-shattering win.

Their top pro, Tyler "Ninja" Blevins, after watching the Retrievers bench flashing those celebratory Fortnite signs for much of the second half, has already given the team a major shout-out on Twitch, the live-streaming platform for gamers.

This leads to a hilarious post-game interview with Nolan Gerrity, the 6-10 junior reserve center with the shock of neon-blond hair, when the media descends on the UMBC locker room.

Asked whether he can put into words what the win over Virginia means to him and his teammates, Gerrity looks into the TV cameras and says with a straight face: "It's like your first victory in Fortnite."

Seeing the puzzled looks on the faces of the reporters, Gerrity doubles down: "We got the no. 1 Fortnite player in the world, Ninja, to (post) about us." Which only leads to more bewildered looks from some of the older media members.

"We're not really this nerdy," freshman forward Brandon Horvath hastens to explain.

Yet they clearly are. Much of the team plays Fortnite seemingly every moment they're not on the court. The nerd factor grows exponentially higher when another reporter asks Gerrity to name UMBC's most successful sports team to date and he mentions the six-time national champion chess team.

"They paved the way," he deadpans.

"We joined the ranks," junior forward Max Portmann adds.

When Ryan Odom and the three seniors return from their interview with Tracy Wolfson, the atmosphere quickly devolves into a mosh-pit-like frenzy, with coaches, players and staff bouncing up and down in the tiny room and yelling like lunatics.

A large cardboard facsimile of the South Regional bracket is brought in by an NCAA rep and the seniors, Lyles, Maura and Grant, perform the ceremonial rite of placing a tape with UMBC's name in the spot reserved for the advancing first round team.

When Odom addresses the team, he pivots deftly from middle-aged metal-head bro to serious coach mode.

He praises the Retrievers lock-down D and calls it the key to the win. ("You defended at a *really* high level.") He lauds their tightness as a unit and their grit. ("You looked out for each other. You were tough as nails. And now you're advancing.")

As he speaks, some players study the floor or shift restlessly from one foot to another. It's not that he's losing the room, necessarily. It's that the vibe is pure joy and pride and relief now. Anything that smacks of soberness and introspection is too hard to process.

"The key is," Odom continues, "you don't have long to get ready for the next" game.

But the next game, a match-up with formidable Kansas State Sunday evening, is far from the Retrievers' thoughts right now. Their coach might as well be urging them to start thinking about their retirement portfolios.

Or when to sign up for Medicare.

No, to these players, all that matters is this heaving emotional catharsis taking place in this moment, a moment they'll remember forever.

It becomes even more indelible when Freeman Hrabowski, smiling beatifically, joins them. Gazing at the happy chaos all around him, he declares: "In 30 years, this is the best day in UMBC history!"

Moments later, Odom, Lyles, Maura and Sherburne are whisked away for the official post-game presser. On the dais, the three players stare out at the sea of reporters and TV cameras with loopy grins on their faces, drinking in yet another moment they've dreamed about all their lives.

In his opening remarks, Odom says: "To have two back-to-back moments – with the America East championship – with our backs against the wall, to come back and win that game and then go toe-to-toe with the no. 1 team in the country . . . I mean it's unbelievable. That's all you can say."

"It's always exciting to make history," Jairus Lyles says, before admitting "I don't think it's really sunk in for us."

K.J. Maura, who has confessed to playing with a heavy heart at times this season, says this win is for his homeland of Puerto Rico, still hurting from Hurricane Maria, the devastating Category 5 storm that slammed into the island six months earlier.

A reporter asks Joe Sherburne: "You had the first six points in the second half to give your team the lead. What was going through your mind . . . when you were knocking down the shots?"

It's then that Sherburne feels the need to share a story about the particular form of grief a Retriever can face when he violates one of Odom's principal dictums: if you've got a good shot, take it.

"In the first half, I passed up a couple of three's," the junior forward explains. "And that really angered my teammates. So in the second half, I made sure I got some off.

"There was one I missed and Arkel got the rebound and passed it right back to me. I thought about doing an extra pass over to K.J.. But I knew everyone was gonna yell at me if I didn't shoot that one, too. So I just let it go."

Watching proudly from the back of the room are Dave Odom and his wife Lynn, as well as Ryan's wife, Lucia, and their youngest son, Owen.

There's another familiar figure with them, too, a grinning teenager talking excitedly with his family and holding up his cell phone to record the giddy scene swirling around him. Connor Odom, six months removed from his last treatment for OCD and feeling better, has never looked happier.

At a little after 1 a.m., Seth Davis, the CBS studio analyst, goes on the network's post-game show and issues a formal apology for his early Sharpie diss of the Retrievers.

"I have egg on my face – a lot of us do," he admits. Which leads to dozens of UMBC supporters taking to social media to gleefully point out that, no, what Davis has on his face is not just a single egg, but more like a giant omelet.

Yet Davis' act of atonement, while noble, is not enough. He has a rep for being one of the good guys in the business, and for not taking himself too seriously. He knows what else must be done in this case.

It's what honorable men do when they screw up, even in the most egregious manner. Sure, they can toss out a public mea culpa. But then they try to make things right. Davis feels the need to do that now.

So it is that in the early hours of the morning, after the most surreal upset in the history of March Madness, Davis takes to his Twitter account to write the two words Retriever Nation has been waiting for:

"UMBC. Sharpie."

Retrievers' guard Jairus Lyles driving for a layup against Virginia. (Mitchell Layton photo.)

Senior guard Jairus Lyles hits the last-second three-pointer over Vermont's Trae Bell-Haynes to give UMBC a 65-62 win in the championship game of the America East Tournament. The victory sent the Retrievers to the NCAA tournament for the first time since 2008. (photo by Brian Jenkins, courtesy America East Conference.)

Players and fans react in the Sports Zone on Selection Sunday as the no. 16-seed Retrievers learn they'll face no. 1-seed Virginia in the first round of the South Regional in Charlotte, N.C.. (Marlayna Demond photo.)

UMBC senior guard K.J. Maura splits the Virginia defense for an easy layup in the second half of the Retrievers shocking 74-54 win over the Cavaliers. (Mitchell Layton photo.)

UMBC coach Ryan Odom calls a play during the game against Virginia. The 42-year-old Odom would go on to win the Hugh Durham award given annually to the mid-majors' top coach. (Mitchell Layton photo.)

A beaming K.J. Maura celebrates with UMBC fans in the waning seconds of the victory that sent the Retrievers into a second-round matchup with Kansas State. (Mitchell Layton photo.)

Exultant Retriever fans at Spectrum Center give the team a rousing ovation as the final horn sounds on the game that will be remembered at UMBC for ages. (Mitchell Layton photo)

Coach Ryan Odom and seniors Jourdan Grant, K.J. Maura and Jairus Lyles are interviewed by TNT sideline reporter Tracy Wolfson after the greatest March Madness upset ever. (Mitchell Layton photo.)

A jubilant Dr. Freeman Hrabowski and his wife, Jacqueline, celebrate the team's big win. UMBC's long-time president authored a moving piece for The Atlantic the next day titled "The Secret of the Greatest Upset in College Basketball History." (UMBC photo.)

UMBC economics professor Nick Kelly and his wife Laura, with their dog Keeper, kiss the True Grit statue on UMBC's campus moments after the Retrievers' victory over the Cavaliers. (Nick Kelly photo.)

UMBC freshman forward Dan Akin gets past Kansas State defender Xavier Sneed for a layup in the Retrievers' 50-43 loss to the Wildcats in the second round of the South Regional. (Mitchell Layton photo.)

A blizzard of confetti rains down on mascot True Grit as the campus honors the history-making Retrievers at the UMBC Event Center a week after their return from Charlotte. (Marlayna Demond photo.)

Retrievers celebrating after upset of Virginia. (Mitchell Layton photo.)

CHAPTER 16

The Agony of Defeat, Redux

• • • •

Charlotte, N.C.

It's around midnight when Virginia coach Tony Bennett and guards Kyle Guy and Ty Jerome make the long death march to the post-game interview room the Retrievers have just vacated.

When they reach the podium, the toll the game has taken on the players is apparent. Jerome looks like he's been hit over the head with a shovel, his eyes vacant and red-rimmed. Guy, shoulders slumped, plops heavily in his seat, grim-faced and sniffling.

Only Bennett, appearing as unruffled as always, looks like his old self. Hair neatly combed, tie perfectly knotted, suit jacket crisp and wrinkle-free, forehead betraying not a hint of perspiration, it's as if he's stepped off the cover of GQ.

Even as the trio settles in behind the microphones, the whispers in Cavaliers Nation are starting already.

Some are questioning, some are critical. Some, predictably, are downright ugly:

Why can't this team win in March? Is it because they're a bunch of chokers? Or is Bennett's offense just too damn plodding and predictable to be effective in the high-pressure, one-and-done atmosphere of the post-season — especially when we're down?

Can Bennett even recruit anymore? Why don't we have a big stud that can put the ball on the floor and go one-on-one and create shots for himself?

The Cavaliers can't run from the fact that they got owned tonight. UMBC is the first team to score 70 points on them all season. Virginia entered the game giving up 53.4 points per game; the Retrieves scored 53 in the second half alone, something no other opponent has managed to do for the past five seasons.

To make things worse, this marks the fourth time in the past five years that the Cavs have been booted from the NCAA Tournament by a lower-seeded team.

A year ago, as the no. 5 seed in the East, they were blown out in the second round by no. 4 Florida, 65-39. In 2016, as the top seed in the Midwest, they lost to no. 10 Syracuse in the Elite 8.

In 2015, as a 2-seed, they lost to 7-seed Michigan State in the third round. And the year before that, as the top seed in the East, they lost to Michigan State, a 4-seed, in the round of 16.

All of that, along with this latest almost-incomprehensible debacle, has the media critics weighing in, too.

"Because of the way (the Cavaliers) play, as great as it is . . . there is a chance for a smaller margin of error" in these tournament games, ESPN analyst Seth Greenberg tells The New York Times.

Jay Bilas, perhaps the most well-known of the network's talking heads, is not nearly as measured in his assessment of this latest March Madness disaster.

"This is the most stunning collapse of a no. 1 team that I've ever seen," he says. "Virginia was very un-Virginia-like. I mean, they were *horrible.*"

Yet as Bennett gazes out at the roomful of reporters - some yawning and borderline cranky due to the late hour, wanting only a quick post-mortem so they can make last call at the nearest watering hole—he's as classy and thoughtful as ever.

In his opening remarks, he congratulates UMBC before choosing to take a 30,000-foot view of what just happened to his team.

And what he says next about losing and perspective and emotional growth might one day be required reading for every 5-star recruit pulling on his new school's basketball uniform for the first time.

"I told these guys in the locker room, you know, a week ago we were cutting down the nets in the ACC Tournament, and how good that felt," Bennett begins. "And they had a historic season . . . and then we had a historic loss, being the first 1-seed to lose. So that's life.

"We talk about it all the time. With the adulation and the praise—it comes and we got a lot of it this year. And then on the other side, there'll be blame and people pointing that out. But that can't define, in the end, these guys or our team.

"If you play this game," he continues, managing to smile, "and you step in the arena, this stuff can happen.

And those who haven't been in the arena, in the competition, maybe they don't understand that."

In contrast to their gracious and eloquent coach, Jerome and Guy seem barely able to process the idea that their season has come to a screeching halt, and that soon enough, they'll be filing silently onto the team bus for the long ride back to Charlottesville.

Jerome, in particular, seems devastated. But he knows there's an autopsy to be gotten through here. Or maybe an inquest is the better term, all with the TV cameras rolling and digital recorders whirring and everyone demanding to know: *what in God's name happened to you guys out there?*

"We didn't pass the ball well," Jerome says in a barely audible voice. "We didn't come off screens. We didn't do anything well, to be honest. And give credit to them, too. They played well."

Guy is only slightly less self-flagellating in his assessment of the ease with which UMBC disrupted Virginia's offense and the outright panic this triggered.

"Defensively, they were very quick, beating the screens . . ." he says. "It was hard to get in a rhythm. And once we got down eight or 10, we were trying to make home run plays."

A vast silence comes over the room, which seems to suit Jerome and Guy just fine. Perhaps they're entertaining the wild notion that this painful grilling might be over, and that they may be excused to go back to their locker room and wallow in their misery with their teammates.

But no, it's far too early for that kind of blessed relief.

A reporter soon raises his hand with this doozy for Jerome: "You listed a bunch of things that were sort of happening about why you guys didn't play well. Do you have any idea *why* it happened that way?"

If it's possible, Jerome looks even more stricken than before.

"You know, it's basketball. You're not going . . ." he offers before his voice trails off. "I mean, I don't know why. I guess we didn't, maybe we didn't come ready to play today . . ."

Even for some grizzled members of this media scrum, used to asking difficult questions of athletes after some of the most heart-breaking moments of their careers, this is becoming hard to watch.

It does not get any easier when, a moment later, a young reporter asks: "What kind of life lesson does this teach both of you?"

From the expressions on their faces, it's clear both players would rather cut off a leg than contemplate whether any particular knowledge or insight has been gleaned from this awful night.

Nevertheless, Jerome gamely attempts an answer.

"Coach Bennett and the staff told us earlier in the year, it's the flip side of the coin," he begins. "The same people who will tell you how great you are and praise you when you're on top of the world, are the same people who will kill you when you're at this point."

He pauses for a moment. Then he feels driven to finish with the thought that hits every player like a slap in the face after a loss like this one, the thought that coaches preach and players ignore until the day comes when they smack their forehead and think: *Wow, Coach was right!*

"It just shows you anybody can beat anybody," Jerome says. "And when you don't come to play, you're gonna get beat. That's basketball."

When it's his turn to answer, Guy seems barely able to speak. He looks down for a full five seconds, clears his throat and seems on the verge of tears.

"It's a blur right now," he begins. Another pause. "It's really hard to answer these questions . . . One thing this team is really good at and built on is resiliency. Bouncing back from something so heart-breaking will be a huge key for us."

Seconds later, the tournament official running the presser delivers the merciful news that the two players are excused.

Leaving their coach to answer a few more questions, Jerome and Guy rise slowly and make their way down a dim hallway to the hushed Virginia locker room, where the ghastly events of the past two-and-a-half hours feel like the worst dream imaginable.

CHAPTER 17

A (Digital) Star Is Born

• • • •

Charlotte, N.C.

It was the English actor Tom Holland who once observed, apropos of something or other: "Fame is a beast that you can't control or be prepared for."

Unbeknownst to Zach Seidel, he's about to discover that that's true.

As the young digital media swami walks to the UMBC locker room, where he's been assigned to monitor post-game interviews, he's greeted by a wondrous sight: a long line of reporters waiting for entry.

As a general rule, media hordes do not materialize after most America East games. Unless you consider a couple of unshaven local scribes and a lone cameraman — with taco sauce stains on his shirt from the halftime spread—to be a horde.

When he reaches the locker room, one of the NCAA reps on hand to keep order smiles and waves him over.

"Hey, can I get a selfie with you?" the man asks.

Now Seidel is truly befuddled.

This is hardly a request that relatively-anonymous computer geeks get every day. Or every 20 years, for that matter.

"Uh, why do you want a selfie?" Seidel asks.

The rep looks at him as if he's lost his mind.

"Dude, you're famous!" he replies. "Your tweets are amazing!"

It's at this point, as he pushes his way into the room, that Seidel's mind begins to churn and he wonders: *What in the hell is going on here?*

What's going on is this: Zach Seidel, a formerly low-profile worker bee for a formerly low-profile university with a formerly low-profile basketball team, has emerged as a genuine Twitter super-nova.

His clever, cheeky in-game posts and the sly burns he directed at haters have earned him a new and massive fan following online. Over the past two hours, the UMBC social media account went from having 5400 followers to more than 41,000. (It will top out at around 111,000 followers before the weekend is through.)

Seidel's posts were re-tweeted 48,000 times, with fans delighting in not just the irreverent shots at Seth Davis, but also the smart, pointed commentary that talked up the "little guy" Retrievers and demanded respect for their play all game long.

Now, as the media swarms the UMBC locker room, Seidel's phone is blowing up.

CNN, ESPN, The New York Times, The Washington Post, USA Today all want to interview him. So do local TV stations in Baltimore and Washington. And sports-talk radio shows around the country.

If Seidel wonders if he's somehow wandered into a bizarre parallel universe, where behind-the-scenes staffers

at college basketball's biggest showcase are suddenly trans-
formed into celebrities, it soon gets even stranger.

That's when an ESPN reporter comes up to him and
says: "So you're the Twitter guy?"

Seidel shrugs.

"I . . . I guess," he says.

But when the reporter asks if he can interview him,
the self-effacing Seidel shuts him down. Suddenly, all this
unwanted attention is starting to weird him out.

"This isn't about me," he tells the reporter. "The guys
are the ones who made the shots. I wasn't out there. I can't
hit a three."

But the reporter will have none of it.

"No, you *are* part of this," he replies. "You *are* part of
the story. Don't you realize that?"

With that, he sticks a microphone with the ESPN flag in
Seidel's face and starts peppering him with questions. And
when other reporters in the crowded room see this—*Hey, is
that the Twitter guy? Giving interviews?*—there is no escape.

Seidel is quickly surrounded by the media jackals
and for the next few minutes, to the vast amusement of
the UMBC players, it's the Twitter Guy who conducts an
impromptu news conference in the midst of a blissed-out
locker room.

The reporters seem eager to learn the secret of how this
beefy digital savant positioned himself to be a social media
phenomenon in the midst of one of the biggest annual
sporting events in the country.

"What was the plan going in?" they want to know.

The plan?

As if Seidel had pulled out his laptop before the opening tip with some kind of brilliant scheme in mind to capture national attention and show off his comedic chops.

There was no *plan*, he tells them. Jairus Lyles needed 15 points to set the Retrievers single-season scoring record. That was the only thing Seidel knew he'd be tweeting out when the game started.

Everything after that was just winging it, he tells them. Just having *fun*.

Some of the reporters still look skeptical, like he's holding something back, some kind of deep, dark secret they can plug into their stories to explain why this guy Seidel – a digital sports dweeb, after all—is getting this kind of worshipful buzz.

But even when the reporters finally let him go and he returns to monitoring player interviews, Seidel's phone doesn't stop ringing.

Malika Andrews of the Times has called twice. So when there's a lull in the media scrum, she gets the first call-back. To do this, he slips into the only quiet place he can find, the shower area, mercifully devoid of naked, celebrating athletes with the locker room still open to reporters.

Finally, over an hour after the game, he checks his phone and sees he's missed five calls from his parents. There is also a text from them. As UMBC grads themselves, Jeff and Nadine Seidel are over the moon with their alma mater's historic win.

But they're also concerned about their inability to reach their youngest son for so long.

"Big win!" the text from his mom reads. "But what's going on with you?"

"Being interviewed," Zach texts back.

"For what?" comes the reply.

"The game," Seidel answers.

"Oh, yeah? Interviewed by who?'

"NY Times, CNN, ESPN," he writes.

"You're full of shit!" she writes back tenderly.

To which Zach responds with something he'd never thought he'd ever say to another human being, let alone a family member: "Google me."

Then still deluged with calls and messages from news outlets and swamped with other responsibilities, he turns off his phone.

When he finally turns it back on, there is another text from a loved one, this one from his sister Kara.

"Holy shit!" it reads. "We Googled you!" Her little brother, she and her parents have discovered, wasn't bull-shitting them at all.

For Seidel, now a full-fledged Twitter phenomenon, it will go on to be the longest night of his still-fledgling career.

He stays up giving interviews to media outlets all over the country until 4:30 in the morning. Not until 6, thoroughly exhausted, does he finally tumble into bed, the TV tuned to ESPN's Sports Center, where the Retrievers' norm-shattering upset will be the no. 1 topic all weekend long.

CHAPTER 18

Free Pizza Looms

• • • •

Catonsville, Md.

On a blustery Saturday some 12 hours after the Retrievers' pull off possibly the biggest upset in sports, the level of excitement on the UMBC campus can best be described as . . . *torpid.*

All in all, it appears to be a great place to take a nap.

There are no smashed windows, flipped cars and mounds of empty beer bottles testifying to a night of boisterous celebrating. If any wild St. Patrick's Day festivities are revving up, they're doing so with a level of secrecy that would shame the NSA.

Dueling message boards speak to the seeming ambivalence with which the student body regards its sports programs, including its now-famous men's basketball team.

One board blares: "Congrats Big Dawgs on making March Madness history!" Yet on the side of The Commons, another sign apprising students of upcoming events announces: "3 14 Pi Day 12 p.m. Main St."

Only after that does it mention − in sort of "oh-yeah-and-there's--this" fashion: "3 16 UMBC vs. UVA 9:20 p.m."

As it happens, Pi Day is essentially a high holy day for math geeks. Celebrated all over the world, it marks the occasion when the numbers in the date (3-14) match the first three digits of the mathematical constant pi, written as π.

On science and tech campuses like UMBC's, Pi Day may feature passionate discussions about pi, pi recitations (who can recite the most digits of the fixed value), readings from "Joy of Pi" by David Blatner and viewings of the Darren Aronofsky film "Pi," about a demented mathematician who believes everything in life can be explained through numbers.

Also encouraged on Pi Day is the actual eating of, well, pie.

Which – in an impossibly cool touch—is given away free.

But Pi Day took place three days earlier. Now the "in" place to be is the library, where UMBC students are doing what they do most often: studying until the blood seeps from their eyeballs.

Here and there, whispered conversations break out about last night's thrilling win over Virginia.

But the chit-chat is kept to a minimum. This, after all, is a serious learning environment. It's where scholars work on research projects that, among other things, rethink global reforestation, recover nutrients from human urine in municipal wastewater, and fabricate wearable temperature-sensing systems for CIPA (Congenital Insensitivity to Pain) patients.

A headline on the New York Times web site captures the campus vibe perfectly: "After Historic Victory, U.M.B.C. Students Look Forward to the Next . . . Lab."

"There are more geese than students roaming the paths on a cold, gray, drizzly Mid-Atlantic afternoon," reads the second paragraph of the Times piece. "Apparently, it's spring break."

The media are roaming all over the place, looking for color stories about the school that has fixated the college basketball world. One enterprising reporter from Sports Illustrated manages to get Dr. Alan Sherman, a professor of computer science and the head of the school's chess program, on the horn.

UMBC, in effect, has become the Duke of college chess, with six national titles since 2003 and 10 Pan American Intercollegiate championships since 1996. As far as the NCAA Tournament goes, Sherman had emailed an old high school friend before last night's game, basically saying he thought Virginia would mop up the floor with the Retrievers.

He was, of course, hardly alone with this opinion. But Sherman seems happy that he was as dead-wrong as Seth Davis.

"I think it's wonderful," he tells the Times reporter of the Retrievers' win. "I don't know how they did it. It's kind of like a novice beating a grandmaster at chess."

To be sure, a small number of folks — alumni, faculty members, residents from the surrounding neighborhoods — have driven to campus in an attempt to soak up any vestiges of excitement left over from the big win the night before.

Others are here to stock up on Retriever gear, including mugs, key-chains, posters and the like. The UMBC bookstore received online orders for some 3,000 T-shirts overnight. But there will be no gleeful memorabilia-shopping today, either. The bookstore is closed.

Instead, most of the poor souls hoping for a dose of Retriever Fever are relegated to wandering over to the statue of True Grit, perhaps thinking they might absorb an aesthetic chill or two left over from last night's merriment.

By now, the 500-pound bronze mascot has been petted, patted, rubbed and smooched so many times you'd expect it to be keeled over on its massive granite slab, panting with exhaustion.

But this new mini-wave of visitors indulges in the same touchy-feely rituals, iPhone cameras clicking away as sons and daughters, mother and fathers, grandmothers and grandfathers strike goofy poses with the solemn-looking dog for posterity.

If the campus itself isn't exactly humming with excitement, it's fair to say the rest of the nation has gone all in on the Retrievers and the incredible underdog story they've authored.

UMBC is mentioned on the front page of the print edition of the Times, where the lead story is a salacious account of a certain orange-haired U.S. president and a porn star. The Washington Post's page 1 tease above the fold reads: "Top-seeded U-Va. wilts in historic first-round loss to UMBC."

Even the august NPR web site blares: "UMBC's Retrievers Put Virginia in a Hole, Then Buried Every Single Bracket."

Ryan Odom and his team are even big news overseas, where the French sports daily L'Equipe trumpets: "UMBC signe l'exploit du siècle dans le tournoi NCAA." ("UMBC marks the feat of the century in the NCAA Tournament.") And before the day is through, Sports Illustrated will unveil a special digital cover commemorating the greatest victory in the school's history.

"Peak Madness" it will say at the top of the page. Underneath will be an arresting photo of last night's hero, no. 10 Jairus Lyles, driving the lane and soaring in a thicket of Virginia defenders to put up a soft floater, further slamming the door on any notion of a Cavaliers' comeback.

"Sweetest 16. UMBC. Just UMBC" is the caption.

A canvas print will set you back $84. A framed print goes for $111. An art print? A steal at a mere 19 bucks.

Finally, there is this: UMBC's big win has caused a financial bloodbath of sorts for Little Caesars Pizza.

Some 24 hours earlier, the country's third-largest pizza chain had run an ad with this tantalizing prospect: "Free lunch combo if crazy happens." The crazy in this case was clearly spelled out: "If a #16 beats a #1 in men's basketball TONIGHT . . ."

Now the crazy has happened. Which means that in a matter of days, much of the nation gets to enjoy a four-slice deep dish pizza and 20-ounce Pepsi Cola product on the house.

"You're welcome, America," tweets @UMBCAthletics, now anticipating an even greater rush to jump on the school's bandwagon.

If there's even any room left.

CHAPTER 19

The Newest America's Team

• • • •

Charlotte, N.C.

If the mood on the UMBC campus is decidedly lethargic, things could not be more festive on the streets of North Carolina's most populous city.

The top tourist attractions here are the NASCAR Hall of Fame, followed by the Billy Graham Library. But today, it's the hundreds of UMBC fans milling about that seems to be the focus of attention.

For one thing, anyone wearing Retrievers gear is accorded near-celebrity status, receiving smiles, waves and warm wishes of good luck. Also passed along are shouted predictions about the team's future, some seemingly un-tethered to reality. ("You guys are going all the way! National championship, bay-bee! We just know it!")

A student worker at the school is stopped by a total stranger in front of Spectrum Center and offered $200 for her Retrievers' hoodie. She turns it down, but confesses to friends: "If I had anything on underneath, I would have done it in a heartbeat."

(While $200 for a used garment might sound extreme, the pricing is relative. On eBay, cheap UMBC foam fingers

155

that were given out at the Midnight Madness season kickoff event are selling for 60 bucks.)

When Zach Seidel takes an Uber from his hotel to get something to eat, the driver notices his UMBC sweatshirt and in a thick Caribbean accent, exclaims: "The miracle basketball school!"

The UMBC pep band, the True Grit mascot and the dance team are invited to join the local St. Patrick's Day parade, drawing loud ovations from the hundreds of spectators crammed onto the sidewalks.

The UMBC players themselves spend much of the day holed up in their hotel rooms, resting. Some of them, wired from both the game, interview demands and seeing themselves all over TV, did not get to sleep until dawn.

Their cell phones continue to blow up, too.

Jairus Lyles reports getting 10,000 new Twitter followers. K.J. Maura tells teammates that he's gotten so many notifications his phone froze. Griff Aldrich, the recruiting and program development honcho, has over 350 text messages. When he finally turned in last night at 3:30, his phone was still buzzing like a swarm of angry hornets.

In the moments after the team's thrilling win over Virginia, there had been some talk among the coaches of confiscating the players' phones. The prospect of already exhausted athletes up all night texting and calling their boys back home instead of sleeping was disturbing.

But ultimately Ryan Odom decided not to take such a drastic measure. Snatching their phones, hell, that would be like depriving your average 19-, 20- and 21-year-olds of oxygen. Instead, he made an impassioned plea for his players to do the right thing on their own.

"It would be a shame to have this win," he told them, "and not prepare for the next game the way you prepared for this one."

We don't want to be done now, he implored. That's not why we're here. We want to move on, don't we?

He was, of course, preaching to the choir. The Retrievers have made it clear all week that they fear no team in this South Regional. Now that they've knocked off the Cavaliers, they're brimming with even more confidence, hardly ready to just call it a weekend and get on a flight home.

Yet the truth is, they're also still caught up in all the hoopla and hysteria of the greatest upset their sport has ever seen. Which means they've actually given little thought to their next opponent, a tough, athletic team in Kansas State.

The same cannot be said of the Las Vegas bookmakers, who have installed the Wildcats as 10-point favorites over the Retrievers. This, of course, represents a heightened level of respect for UMBC, which was a 20 ½-point underdog to the Cavaliers.

But the Wildcats are big and strong and play lock-down defense. The bookies know – or at least sense – that it'll be hard for the Retrievers to again summon the same level of energy and aggressiveness they used to beat Virginia.

Still, at the moment, they're such a feel-good national story that they're even dominating the news conferences of other teams here in Charlotte.

When North Carolina players Luke Maye, Kenny Williams and Cameron Johnson sit down at Spectrum Center to talk about their upcoming second-round game against Texas A&M, they're soon peppered with questions about UMBC.

"How surprised were you with (the result of) the Virginia game?" a reporter asks midway through the presser.

"I was actually really surprised," says Williams, the junior guard, in what does not exactly qualify as a stunning revelation. "UMBC did a great job knowing what they wanted to do: driving and kicking and then knocking down the shots."

He pauses and grins, as if still dumb-founded at the memory. "They just executed their game plan perfectly."

Yet when all three Tar Heels are asked if they're familiar with anyone on the UMBC roster—anyone at all—they shake their heads no.

After some contemplation, Maye, a junior forward, finally offers up that Ryan Odom, then an assistant coach at UNC-Charlotte, expressed interest in recruiting him out of high school. And Williams remembers – well, sort of— talking to Jairus Lyles at VCU, back when Williams was considering playing for Shaka Smart, before the coach bailed for Texas.

And *still* the questions about UMBC keep coming.

To their credit, Maye, Williams and Johnson handle them with equanimity, betraying no outward sign of resentment. They recognize that a transformational event has occurred in their sport, one that had long been anticipated, but that feels mind-boggling now nonetheless.

"What do you think it means to those guys to first make the tournament and then pull off history?" another reporter asks Johnson of the Retrievers.

The redshirt junior forward grins and nods knowingly.

"They gotta be on cloud nine right now," he says. "To pull off something like that . . ."

His voice trails off. Yet in the next instant, another thought occurs: "They got another game coming up. So they can't fly too high."

That, essentially, is what most concerns Ryan Odom now, the idea that the past 24 hours have been so exhilarating it'll prevent his players from focusing on what lies ahead.

Odom himself had been up until 4 a.m., huddling with his assistant coaches, watching film of the Wildcats and formulating the game plan for Sunday. Even in that early morning meeting, there was no escaping just how big UMBC was now in the national consciousness.

That was driven home to everyone in the room when Eric Skeeter's cell phone rang at 2:30 in the middle of the skull session. Someone was trying to Facetime him.

Uh-uh, Skeeters thought. *I'm a little busy here.* He ignored it.

But the phone rang again. Same thing: Facetime request. He ignored it again. The phone rang a third time. *What the hell?!*

But now Skeeters glanced down to see who was calling. It was Mark Karcher.

Karcher was the sublime player who led Baltimore's St. Francis Academy to three straight Catholic League titles in the mid-90's, back when Skeeters was an assistant coach at the hoops powerhouse.

When Skeeters told Odom who was calling, the head coach smiled.

"Oh, that's your guy!" he said. "You gotta take it!"

And when Skeeters did, there was Karcher, calling from the Horseshoe Casino in Baltimore and bellowing "I TOLD YOU! THAT'S MY COACH! I TOLD YOU!" while a crowd of some 40 people behind him—many displaying varying levels of sobriety – cheered and shouted "YEAHHH! GO UMBC!"

Skeeters was wildly appreciative. But a minute or two later, he told Karcher he had to get back to work.

"I got you, Coach!" Karcher replied brightly. "Just wanted you to see the love you're getting from Baltimore!"

By the time Odom and Jairus Lyles are interviewed later that morning by Charles Barkley, Odom marvels that the media's voracious interest in his team, far from being sated the previous night, had been turbocharged to a whole new level.

It's like on "American Idol"! he thinks. *Everyone wants you to do something!*

That afternoon, the Retrievers go through a light practice at nearby Queens University, followed by a shoot-around at the Spectrum Center.

This is followed by yet another session with reporters, who have clearly not exhausted all their questions – ranging from the incisive to the dopey—for the nation's newest sports darlings.

"What's something you want people to know about your team?" Joe Sherburne is asked.

As it happens, this one is right up Sherburne's alley.

He has something he needs to get off his chest. In news report after news report following UMBC's unprecedented win, he's seen his team referred to repeatedly as the Golden Retrievers.

This has been enough to make him gag every time. And now, with the media seemingly transfixed on even the most arcane details about his school, he has an opportunity to set the record straight.

To dispel, once and for all, this terrible slander that has been making the rounds.

"We're the Chesapeake Bay Retrievers, *not* the Golden Retrievers," Sherburne says pointedly, going on to elucidate the differences in color (dark brown vs. flaxen) and coat texture (thick and waterproof vs. stringy and knot-prone) between the two breeds.

Although he *could*, he does not get into the contrast in temperament (quietly independent vs. nauseatingly friendly) between the dogs. Nor does he add that his team is also definitely *not* the Labrador Retrievers, which tend to get so wound up their owners sometimes fantasize about putting sedatives in their pet's dish, just to get a moment's peace.

But if we're the biggest thing in the game right now, Sherburne thinks, *if you're gonna talk about us and write about us, at least get the name right.*

If the Retrievers are showing a little extra swagger as the day wears on, so is the @UMBCAthletics account.

161

This, again, comes in the person of Zach Seidel, who feels now is the perfect time to avenge an insult directed at his school months earlier.

Back when the University of Maryland routed UMBC 66-45 in a game at College Park in December, a Terrapins fan had tweeted a photo of himself holding a sign that said: "University of Maryland Back-up College."

Now, like some digital *mafiosi* who's been waiting for the perfect time to strike back for the awful slur, Seidel re-tweets the photo.

Only this time it's accompanied with an appropriately cutting caption: "Hopefully you enjoyed our game from your couch dude!"

CHAPTER 20

Let the Debate Begin

• • • •

Charlotte, N.C.

In the hours since the Retrievers pulled off the "Shocker in Charlotte," the pundits scramble to give context to the story – and to determine where it ranks among the all-time greatest sports upsets.

The consensus opinion of many: right at the top.

A 20-point rout of the top-ranked team in the NCAA Tournament?

By a lowly 16-seed?

Representing a mid-major school the vast majority of college basketball fans had never heard of?

Please. If you tried selling that to Hollywood, you'd be laughed out of the pitch meeting within seconds.

"It's a story writers couldn't dream up to write," Dave Odom, Ryan's dad, tells reporters. "You just couldn't write it. If you did, nobody would buy it. Because they wouldn't think it's true."

Yet with no. 16 seeds previously being 0-for-135 against no. 1's since the beginning of time – OK, since 1985, when the tournament grew to 64 teams – how could this not be one of the most extraordinary underdog stories ever?

163

"You know what this is like?" a reporter for USA Today overhears the CBS analyst Bill Raftery telling people. "This is like saying, 'Well, you know, one day the aliens are going to land here and that's going to be incredible.' But in the back of your mind you're like 'C'mon, man, we all know the aliens are never going to land here.'"

Cody Benjamin of cbssports.com shoots the Retrievers right to no. 1 on his list of greatest upsets.

"The score of this game – UMBC 74, Virginia 54 – wasn't even close," he writes, "but that only solidifies how insane this was."

He ranks the USA's hockey team's "Miracle on Ice" win over the Soviet Union in the 1980 Winter Olympics no. 2. It's a solid choice. Set against the backdrop of the Cold War, the grizzled Russian pros, who had won the gold medal in five of the six previous Winter Games, were expected to wipe the ice with the young, wide-eyed, just-happy-to-be-here American amateurs.

Instead, Coach Herb Brook's plucky squad held on for a thrilling 4-3 win watched by the entire nation, culminating in announcer Al Michaels' iconic call: "Do you believe in miracles?! YES! Unbelievable!"

Benjamin's no. 3 choice for biggest upset is not so conventional, however. Here he lists Harvard knocking off Stanford in the first round of the 1998 women's NCAA basketball tournament.

This was the first time a no. 16 seed beat a no. 1 seed in all of D-1 hoops, so the linkage to UMBC over Virginia is undeniable. But the Crimson women won by only four points (71-67). And even though Stanford had won two national championships and been to six Final Fours in the previous eight seasons, the team was missing its two stars, Vanessa Nygaard and Kristin Folkl, due to serious knee injuries.

Bryan Armen Graham of The Guardian also considers the Retrievers' win to be the biggest upset ever.

"All UMBC won on Friday was a second-round date with Kansas State on Sunday," he writes. "But there was something about no. 16 over no. 1, one of the last things in sports that had never, ever happened, that took on a mythology of its own and made natural fodder for barroom debates: the sort of psychic blockade once associated with the four-minute mile and the sound barrier.

"One day it could happen, we told ourselves year after year, even as it felt less and less likely with each passing tournament."

Henry Bushnell of Yahoo Sports has the "Miracle on Ice" win as his greatest upset, followed by Buster Douglas' incredible knockout of Mike Tyson, for which he, too, makes a compelling case.

"Not only had Tyson never lost when he stepped into the ring against Douglas in 1990," Bushnell writes, "of his 37 wins in 37 fights, 35 had been by knockout. He had a longer and more comprehensive track record of dominance than anybody else on this list.

"That's why Douglas was a 42/1 underdog, and even those odds were, according to reports, only offered at one or a few Las Vegas casinos. It was a foregone conclusion that Tyson would make quick work of his over-matched opponent. And then, well, he didn't."

Bushnell ranks Mississippi State over UConn in the 2017 Final Four in women's basketball as his third greatest upset, noting the Huskies held a 111-game winning streak going in.

Only after that, at no. 4, does he deign to list UMBC over Virginia.

"What made it so remarkable was the margin of victory," he writes. ". . . In a way, though, the thoroughness of the victory downplays how great an upset it was. UMBC would have been able to pull it off even with a flawed performance.

"So while it will go down in college hoops history, it doesn't quite top the all-sports charts."

From all across the country, fans inspired by the Retrievers' win take to social media with their own favorites for greatest upset ever.

Many mention the New York Jets' incredible 16-7 victory over the mighty Baltimore Colts in Super Bowl III. Considered the game that lifted the fledgling AFL from its perceived bush league status to parity with the established NFL, it was high-lighted by New York's brash quarterback, Joe Namath, guaranteeing a Jets victory beforehand.

Others cite the New York "Miracle Mets," an expansion team just eight years earlier, beating the Baltimore Orioles in the 1969 World Series. Still others mention Leon Spinks, a 10-to-1 underdog with eight professional bouts to his credit, winning a split decision over the great Muhammad Ali for the heavyweight boxing title in 1978.

Also weighing in are New York Giants fans, who insist their team's 17-14 win over the undefeated 18-0 New

England Patriots in the 2008 Super Bowl – the G-Men were 12-point underdogs, no less! – is the most shocking upset of all time.

Even a sport as esoteric as Greco-Roman wrestling comes up in the debate, with fans recalling the USA's Rulon Gardner's improbable win over Russia's Alexander Karolin for the gold medal in the 2008 Summer Olympics.

(Karolin had been undefeated in 13 years of international competition. He also hadn't given up a single point in the six years before facing Gardner.)

Some giddy Retrievers supporters even discount Dave Odom's opinion that their team's underdog saga is too fantastical to make it to the big screen.

They liken UMBC's wildly-improbable win to ultimate palooka Rocky Balboa beating Apollo Creed in "Rocky 2." Or to crabby Morris Buttermaker's rag-tag team beating the haughty Yankees in "Bad News Bears." Or to the previously down-on-their luck Ducks beating the Hawks in "The Mighty Ducks."

For others, the Retrievers astonishing upset is the modern-day reincarnation of "Hoosiers," the beloved film based loosely—OK, *very* loosely – on tiny Milan High, with just 161 students, beating powerful Muncie Central in the 1954 Indiana state basketball championships.

Weighing in for Bleacher Report, Tom Weir, who has covered scores of NCAA tournament games and 15 Final Fours in his long career, claims that what happened at Spectrum Center last night is the essence of what makes sports so riveting: their utter unpredictability.

"As university acronyms go, UMBC isn't exactly up there with UCLA, LSU or MIT," he writes. "But the world is rapidly learning about the team with a comma in its name, University of Maryland, Baltimore County.

"The Retrievers – yes Retrievers – might sound like PETA's weekend softball team. But on Friday, they fetched a victory that will forever define them as best of show in the underdog division."

CHAPTER 21

This Is Who We Are

• • • •

Charlotte, N.C.

While the UMBC players rest and try mightily to come down from their emotional high of the past 12 hours and focus on Kansas State, Freeman Hrabowski is consumed with a far different task.

The UMBC president is also running on fumes. He was up all night answering emails and text messages, and receiving congratulatory phone calls and voice mails.

An ecstatic Maryland governor Larry Hogan checked in, crowing that he was the only person in the whole country who picked the Retrievers to win. Speaker of the Maryland House of Delegates Michael Busch sang some sort of sports ditty over the phone. (Predictably, UMBC's leader, the self-professed mega-nerd, didn't recognize the tune. The quality of the Speaker's singing voice is already a blur, too.)

Patrick G. O'Shea, the president of the University of Cork, also reached out. Possibly after already consuming a Guinness or two, he wrote: "Freeman, we are celebrating this great victory in Ireland on St. Patrick's Day!"

It's little wonder Hrabowski didn't get to sleep until after 6 a.m., and awoke just a few hours later. There will be little rest for him today, either. He's caught up in the same media whirlwind as his basketball team, giving interviews to The New York Times, The Washington Post and CNN among other news outlets.

As UMBC's foremost evangelist since taking over as president in 1992, he's also been contacted by The Atlantic and asked to write an essay — on deadline, no less—about what the win over Virginia means for his school.

Hrabowski's enormous pride in the university is palpable whenever he speaks. Now, hunched over a laptop while holed up in his hotel room, he's determined to take advantage of the white-hot media spotlight trained on UMBC to let the world know: *This is who we are.*

For years, UMBC made U.S. News & World Report's list of top up-and coming schools in the nation. The magazine eventually got rid of the gimmick. But it became a running joke on campus: How much longer before they actually see we've up and come?

This is what he hopes to show with his article.

What Hrabowski is most proud of is the diversity on his campus, and the number of black and brown students the predominantly white school attracts to its programs for math, science, technology and engineering. (It leads the nation in the number of African-Americans who go on to get combined M.D.-Ph.D degrees.)

Of the UMBC players on the court last night, as well as the dance team, pep band and the school's fans in the stands, he thinks: *We looked like America. The most privileged places, when you look at the audience, you mainly see privileged people and mainly white people. That's just the way it is.*

What you saw with our crowd was America. We've got people from 100 different countries at our school!

And for the Retrievers to go up against mighty Virginia, one of the oldest and wealthiest public universities in the country, a school founded by Thomas Jefferson, with a giant endowment ($9.6 billion) that dwarfs UMBC's (less than $100 million) and a legendary basketball program – and to come out with a win! – well, the symbolism is overwhelming.

You could look into the Virginia crowd, he thinks, *and see Southern aristocracy. All that wealth was readily apparent. The significance of the UMBC story is, it's saying to the country: you don't have to be rich as a person or an institution to become the very best.*

Hrabowski's own personal history makes him uniquely qualified to talk about disparities in education – and in life – brought on by racial prejudice and wealth inequities.

He grew up in segregated Birmingham, AL., in the 1950's and 1960's, in the same neighborhood as Condoleezza Rice, the former Secretary of State in the George W. Bush administration. Black children back then were constantly reminded that their lives were not as valued as white children.

The schools of black kids were inferior to the ones in white neighborhoods. Their textbooks were throwaways from white students. Black children were barred from the local amusement park.

They were forced to sit in the sweltering balconies of movie theaters, shunted away from white patrons in restaurants, forced to endure humiliating waits in stores while white customers were waited on first. Separate drinking

171

fountains were omnipresent reminders of their second-class citizenship.

In May of 1963, as a 12-year-old, young Freeman marched for civil rights in Dr. Martin Luther King's Children's Crusade. A poignant speech King delivered weeks earlier in a local church spurred Freeman and many other kids to action.

"He made the point that children could be empowered to help shape their destiny," Hrabowski would recall years later. "They can be a part of this democracy, even as a 12-year-old. That was so powerful."

The march, with almost a thousand students, kicked off at Birmingham's 16th Street Baptist Church, bound for City Hall. Organizers had prepared the children as best they could for the humiliations and dangers that lay ahead. Jittery city fathers, having denied the marchers a permit to assemble peacefully, ordered police to use snarling German Shepherds, powerful fire hoses and baton-wielding officers to break up the demonstration.

Hundreds were arrested along the way, but young Freeman and some cohorts made it to the steps of City Hall. There they were confronted by Eugene "Bull" Connor, the notorious commissioner of public safety and arch-segregationist, steaming mad because TV cameras were present, recording the chaos for the rest of a shocked nation.

As recounted in Hrabowski's 2015 book "Holding Fast to Dreams," Connor singled out Freeman for interrogation.

"He looked at me and said 'What do you want, little Nigra?'" Hrabowski wrote. "Remember, I was not a courageous kid. I looked up at him, scared, and managed to say, in my Birmingham accent, 'Suh, we want to kneel and pray.'

"He spat in my face. Then my fellow demonstrators and I were gathered up and shoved into a police wagon waiting nearby."

Young Freeman would spend five days in jail with scores of his fellow marchers.

"It was an abomination," he declared years later. "We were treated like animals. There were not enough bathrooms. It was smelly. We were hungry. It was awful."

The children 14 and older were remanded to a different facility. As a 12-year-old entering his sophomore year in high school – his keen intellect and voracious appetite for education helped him skip two grades – Freeman was designated as a leader of his group of child prisoners.

To calm the other boys, many of them crying for their mothers, he read the Bible to them and organized games. As he recounts in his book, making the stay behind bars even more terrifying was the fact they'd been thrown in with older juvenile delinquents being punished for real crimes.

"The guards encouraged these boys to be verbally and physically intimidating and abusive," he wrote. "We could hear kids hollering in other cells. Unspeakable things happened."

Dr. King and the parents of the frightened boys held a vigil outside the detention center later, during which the reverend tried to boost their spirits.

"We were all crying, but Dr. King assured us that our participation in the march and our going to jail would help make the world a better place for children not yet born,"

Hrabowski wrote. "And though we may not have fully grasped the profound significance of that statement, his words gave us strength and invited us to think about the possibilities."

Now, as he labors over The Atlantic essay he's titled "The Secret Behind the Greatest Upset in College Basketball History," he decides what the world needs to know most of all about UMBC is this: it's stunning upset of Virginia vividly reflects how "unabashedly aspirational" the school is.

" People now know the University of Maryland, Baltimore County, as the ultimate Cinderella, an overnight media sensation, the team that magically emerged as the first No. 16 seed to defeat a No. 1 in the history of the NCAA Men's Basketball Tournament," he begins.

"But our story is far less fairy tale than it is classic American dream. Our magic comes from questioning expectations, putting in the hard work, and staying focused."

Over some 1500 words, UMBC's president lays out a compelling case that the Retrievers' historic upset springs directly from the conviction, espoused everywhere on campus, that to set limits on human beings is folly.

"Everybody thought it couldn't be done because it hadn't been done," he writes. "And then we did it."

Only briefly in the Atlantic piece does he mention the turmoil in his Deep South hometown when he was growing up, and his small part in fighting for justice. But it's not hard to see that the unwavering hope that sustained him as a youth, that led him to overcome Birmingham's naked racism and graduate from Hampton University at 19, get

174

his doctorate from the University of Illinois at Urbana-Champaign at 24 and become one of America's foremost academics, is not dissimilar to the hope the Retrievers carried – against all odds—at Spectrum Center Friday night.

"I learned you don't give up," Hrabowski will say of all he endured and overcame. "And that resiliency matters. And you keep dreaming."

Now, after finishing his essay and pushing send on his laptop, the dream he focuses on involves his beloved Retrievers.

In less than 24 hours, they'll be in the national spotlight once again. Dominating the best team in the country as a 16-seed and following that with another huge upset, this time over no. 9 Kansas State to elbow your way into the Sweet 16—that's about as "unabashedly aspirational" as it gets.

CHAPTER 22

A Genuine Mob Scene

* * * *

Catonsville, Md.

As Sunday morning dawns, much of Retriever Nation is infused with the kind of audacious hope the school preaches.

There's a growing belief that this gritty basketball team is destined for more than just historic first-round greatness. That it's peaking at just the right time and it's young, savvy head coach is pushing all the right buttons for a deep run in the tournament.

That the indomitable Jairus Lyles, playing with a breath-taking swagger, will again summon the scoring magic that has carried the Retrievers the past two games. That K.J. Maura, artfully shredding traps and presses and disrupting opponents' offensive sets by nipping at the heels of taller guards like a crazed fox terrier, is a secret weapon that will atomize any opponent that takes him lightly.

The promising message "Why Not Us?" on the back of Melvin Maura's T-shirt Friday night has become the mantra for many UMBC fans. *Who says we can't beat Kansas State? Is there any law that says you can't pull off two spectacular upsets in the same tournament?*

The pundits and prognosticators, on the other hand, are all over the place on who will win this game.

"Luckily for the Retrievers," writes The Washington Post, "one of the 11 losses Kansas State suffered this season came against a team that shares UMBC's penchant for a free-flowing offense, perimeter shooting and turnover generation: Arizona State, which forced the typically sure-handed Wildcats into 16 turnovers.

". . .If Lyles continues his torrid shooting pace and they can force Kansas State into the same mistakes Arizona State did, UMBC could be a Sweet 16 team for the ages."

SBnation.com also seems upbeat about the Retrievers' chances.

"If a team is capable of not just beating the no. 1 overall team in the tournament, but destroying them by 20," a story on the web site begins, "then it stands to reason that the same team has at least a puncher's chance to keep advancing in the Big Dance."

The article goes on to list three reasons for Retrievers fans to be optimistic:

Lightly-regarded 15-seed Florida Gulf Coast soundly beat no. 2 seed Georgetown in the 2013 tournament and followed that up with another drubbing, this time of no. 7 San Diego State, two days later. Like the Eagles, UMBC looks fully capable of pulling off more than one upset in the tourney.

Kansas State's two leading scorers, Dean Wade (16.5 point per game) and Barry Brown (16.0 ppg) are banged up.

Judging how Virginia only got to the free throw line eight times Friday night, Kansas State probably won't do much better in getting the Retrievers in foul trouble.

But others are not as bullish about UMBC's prospects of again defying the odds and coming away with a win.

The Heartland College Sports blog writes: "Kansas State doesn't want to 'pull a Virginia.' UMBC cannot hide, and the Wildcats will take this game seriously. With more talent and depth, the Wildcats should easily dispatch UMBC.

"The Retrievers element of surprise is long gone and the absolute circus of attention they've received in the past 24 hours will prove too much to handle for a short turn-around against a veteran Power 5 team."

And cbssports.com, citing numbers from the gambling site SportsLine, is even more dismissive of the Retrievers' quest to make it past the Wildcats:

"SportsLine's advanced computer model, which entered the second round of the 2018 NCAA Tournament on a blistering 5-1 run on spread picks, simulated Kansas State vs. UMBC 10,000 times.

"What it found out: UMBC only has a 14 per cent chance of pulling out its second straight upset win."

On campus, another watch party is planned for The Commons tonight, with far more students expected to attend than attended Friday night, even with spring break still on. The rumor is they're breaking out black and yellow jelly beans for this one, as well as cookies decorated with Retriever faces.

And this party, like the earlier one, will again feature that most UMBC-ish of phenomena, one that annoys the crap out of hard-core March Madness fans: students doing homework or studying for exams as they watch the game.

The UMBC book store, which was closed Saturday, now has all the calm of a Whole Foods with a blizzard on the way. The store received 3,000 on-line orders for T-shirts overnight; by comparison, only 1500 were sold in all of the previous year.

Special T-shirts that say "All Bark and All Bite!" and "We Are History" and the 74-54 score of the Virginia game have been ordered, but haven't come in yet. Which is just as well, since the sight of fresh boxes of Retrievers apparel being ripped open by store employees might trigger a melee in the hyped-up crowd.

When Nick Kelly, the UMBC economics professor and super-fan, arrives at the store around 11, he sees some 75 people lined up before the place has even opened. Once inside, he's forced to navigate scrums of jabbering, wild-eyed souvenir-seekers as he looks for a pennant for his mother.

"It was a mob scene," Kelly will say later, "with people grabbing every single thing they could: shirts, hats, mugs. Things were flying off the shelves. It was something I never thought I'd see."

It's not just the book store bracing for a nice little windfall from the Retrievers success so far. The sense that the school has a chance to cash in on its suddenly soaring national profile is beginning to occur to others in the UMBC administration.

In the middle of the afternoon, @UMBCAthletics sends out this tweet: "BTW guys, we have a brand new $85 million Event Center we opened up last month that still doesn't have a corporate sponsor name . . ."

Is this a joke? Is it a serious overture to Big Business? It turns out to be a little of both, the result of a light-hearted brainstorming session between school veep Greg Simmons and digital wiz Zach Seidel.

The two are in the lobby of the team hotel in Charlotte, reflecting on the Retrievers new-found fame, when Simmons says: "This is a great marketing opportunity. Why don't you subtly mention that we just opened our new arena? And we're looking for a sponsor?"

Seidel whips out his phone and says: "I can probably do it right now. And be really blunt."

Blunt it is, then. Within seconds of his tweet, suggestions pour in from the Twitterverse as to what corporate sponsors the school should hit up.

Many, predictably, are doggie-centric: Petco, Purina, PetSmart, Chewy, etc. One wag even thinks a certain world-renowned rapper should be approached, since Snoop Dog Arena rolls off the tongue.

There are suggestions to contact the Fortnite people, or Lance Snacks, makers of the rejuvenating crackers that kept a cramping Jairus Lyles upright against Virginia.

But on this day, only one company gets back to @ UMBCAthletics: Chicago-based Dude Products, Inc.

Advertising itself as offering "futuristic hygiene for dudes," it seems eager to ink a contract with the school, long-term or otherwise.

Its tweet reads simply: "Dude Wipes Arena. Where do we sign?"

CHAPTER 23

Sleep is Over-Rated

• • • •

Charlotte, N.C.

Meanwhile, more cars and busses filled with UMBC students and fans are rumbling down I-95 toward North Carolina, hopeful of scoring last-minute tickets to the Kansas State game on-line or at Spectrum Center

If worse comes to worse, some might even take their chances with the shaky-looking scalpers that materialize from the shadows at all big events, a breed of entrepreneurs noted for their uncanny ability to sweet-talk (OK, bullshit) customers while having one eye peeled for more business and the other for the cops.

James Wiggins, a 1975 UMBC grad and Baltimore attorney, is one of those making the journey south. He's one of the school's significant boosters, and one of the Retrievers biggest fans, a constant and reassuring presence on game-days as he cheers enthusiastically from his court-side seats.

Much as he does at home games, Wiggins will stand out in the crowd tonight. For this game against K-State, he plans to break out a gold Retriever Nation T-shirt of a luminance that could be seen from the International Space Station.

This is Wiggins' second trip down 95 in the last few days. He drove to Charlotte with a friend and watched the Retrievers thrilling destruction of Virginia, soaking in all the joy and utter madness of that wonderful occasion. But with a hotel room for only one night and no ticket for the Sunday game against Kansas State, he drove back to Baltimore Saturday.

On the ride home, he got a call from Greg Simmons, the school's vp. Simmons had news: there were tickets available for the K-State game.

"Want any?" he asked.

Absolutely, answered Wiggins. Give me two.

And so it is that after making the six-hour ride home and grabbing a few hours sleep, he again sets off this morning for the Tar Heel State. This time he's accompanied by his wife, Evangeline, the two of them grateful for another opportunity to don their dazzling T-shirts and see if their team can't make this dream-like weekend last a little longer.

On one of the UMBC buses headed to Charlotte is Zoe Pekins, a sophomore midfielder on the women's lacrosse team.

Like so many enjoying the wild ride Jairus Lyles and Co. are taking them on, Pekins is sleep-deprived. She was up late Friday night watching the Retrievers shock all of sports, celebrating with her two roommates while marveling at how much better this version of the Retrievers is compared to the hapless crew that lost 25 games her freshman year.

Early the next day, she jumped on a bus with her lacrosse teammates for the four-hours-plus ride to Farmville, Virginia and a game against Longwood University. After notching a 13-10 win, their coach asked if anyone was interested in attending the men's game against K-State the next day.

Definitely, Pekins said. Who needs sleep?

So after the long bus ride back to campus, she arose early this morning for an even longer bus ride to Charlotte. But everyone is excited, and they pass the time taking photos and insisting to any gawkers who approach at rest stops that, yes, this is the famous UMBC basketball team's bus.

And, yes, we're the basketball team. *Maybe a little shorter than you envisioned. And maybe that's disappointing. But, yeah, we're it.*

Pekins and her lacrosse buddies will end up watching the game from the nosebleed seats at Spectrum Center—so high up that if you stand too quickly, you could bang your head on the ceiling and black out.

But before they head inside, they're caught up in the same bizarre exchange others wearing UMBC black and gold have experienced this weekend.

Walking around in their team-issued leggings and long-sleeved hooded sweatshirts, they're approached by a family that quickly offers each woman $150 for her clothes.

Uh, no, Pekins thinks, alarm bells clanging in her head as she considers the NCAA violations such an exchange would trigger. We're here to have fun and support the basketball team, not end up in rules-and-regulations jail.

If folks on the streets of Charlotte are this desperate for Retrievers gear, you wonder what they'd shell out for what Cara Jaye will be modeling tonight.

Jaye, the True Grit mascot performer, is having an absolutely wonderful weekend. She was getting ready to go to an acting class in New York when she received a text from the UMBC marketing people asking if she'd be interested in playing True Grit in Charlotte.

A chance to perform before a national TV audience?

In the biggest gig of her mascot career?

She hesitated two seconds before saying: Count me in. And now, looking back on the past 36 hours and this frenetic weekend, it was one of the best decisions she ever made.

It only gets better when she finds out that for tonight's game, she'll be showing off a new fashion accessory that will go wonderfully with her thick fur outfit and gigantic dog head, with the floppy ears the size of ceiling-fan blades.

It's a special T-shirt given to her by the team, the same T-shirt the players will wear when they take the floor for warm-ups against Kansas State.

"Unleash Chaos" it says on the front. "Shock the World" is on the back.

Street value in Charlotte for the masses clamoring for Retrievers paraphernalia? Who knows? Maybe priceless.

Also having a terrific time in the Queen City is Alexander Jones, a senior and trumpet player in the UMBC Down and Dirty Dawg Band that rocked the house Friday night and plans to again tonight.

Jones is hard to miss. At 6-2 and 270 pounds, he's built along the lines of a stand-up freezer. Band members wear jeans and black Under Armour T-shirts adorned with gold paw prints.

Jones accessorizes his look with a black-and-gold ban-dana and black-and-yellow Converse sneakers with UMBC stitched on it, as well as his graduation year. Sometimes he wears face-paint, too. The total effect is somewhere between menacing biker and pro wrestling villain.

Which turns out to be a fitting look for the occasion. Because as the Dawg Band warms up at Spectrum Center in the dead hours before tonight's game, members of the K-State band approach and begin talking some serious trash.

Their lead trumpet player, a slight woman, is particu-larly irritating.

"Yeah," she announces in a casual voice, "when we move on, we're going to be taking pictures with the other trumpet sections too."

"What do you mean?" one of the Dawgs asks. Although what she means is, of course, painfully obvious.

"Well," she answers, "you guys don't really think you're going to win tonight, do you?"

The chutzpah of this woman astounds the Dawgs.

On the one hand they think: *OK, we must be relevant. Because if we weren't, they wouldn't be talking shit to us.* On the other hand, the disrespect oozing from this person must not go unanswered.

What follows is some predictable jawing back and forth, which gets heated at times. But luckily it goes no further than that, sparing early arriving fans the unsettling sight of a full-on brawl, with rival musicians angrily flailing away at each other with various brass, woodwind and percussion instruments.

CHAPTER 24

Hey, We Can Beat Them

• • • •

Charlotte, N.C.

In the hours before the Retrievers will board the bus for the ride to Spectrum Center, Dana Thomas walks into the team hotel, fresh from her flight from Manchester, New Hampshire.

Thomas is the mother of Max Curran, the 6-9 sophomore reserve who's fought through injuries to play a key role as a rebounder, defender and offensive spark for the team. Spotting Eric Skeeters and Nate Dixon in the lobby, Thomas marches up to them and clears her throat.

"Coaches," she begins, "I just want you to know Max is probably going to be tired today."

Skeeters and Dixon look at each other.

"Oh? Skeeters says finally. "Why is that?"

Thomas explains that her son is likely not feeling tip-top because he was up until at least 2:45 A.M. the previous night. She knows this because she's been monitoring his Twitter account. And he was still posting at that ungodly hour instead of doing what he should have been doing, which was sleeping.

Curran will not find out until later that he's been ratted out by his mom and undone by the social media trail he's

189

left behind. But hearing the news of their player's late-night activities, Skeeters and Dixon can only shrug.

They know it's a good bet that Max wasn't the only team member still caught up in all the hullaballoo swirling around the Retrievers. Not the only one failing to get enough rest, either.

But there's not much the coaches can do about it now. What are the options? Order the kid to take a nap? Ha, good luck suggesting that to a wired 19-year-old in the midst of probably the most thrilling weekend he's ever had, a March Madness odyssey that will end God knows how and when.

Fortunately, when the Retrievers meet for their team meal, there's little evidence any of them are truly sleep-deprived. They perk up even further upon hearing a surprise announcement: a couple of Fortnite executives, one of the game's creators and another from marketing, are coming to their hotel to hang out.

The company headquarters is nearby and everyone there is smitten with UMBC's Cinderella story, not to mention the free publicity the bench guys delivered with their Fortnite dances Friday.

Ryan Odom, meeting with his coaches, is not exactly thrilled when news of the visit is relayed to him. He'd much prefer that his team focus on Kansas State instead of a couple of video game big-shots. But it's never been his style to limit his team's activities and keep the players from things they enjoy doing.

That's why he never seriously thought about taking their cell phones away after the Virginia win. Sure, maybe it would have ensured a better night's sleep for them. But it would have been an uncharacteristic move on his part and they would have been puzzled by it.

Now, with the Fortnite execs on their way, he thinks: *I want the players to experience everything about this tournament without it being a distraction. But there's already so much stuff going on and vying for their attention. So we just have to roll with this and let it happen.*

Unfortunately for the hard-core UMBC players, "Ninja" Blevins, the pro gamer extraordinaire, is a no-show. His schedule is simply too hectic. He might be a little tuckered out, too. Fortnite is the most popular video game in the world and Ninja has just come off a marathon contest with the rapper Drake that attracted a record 388,000 viewers on the streaming service Twitch.

Ninja does, however, Facetime the Retrievers, telling them how dope it is that they're into gaming video games. After that, the players happily spend time peppering the Fortnite guys with questions—*How did you come up with the game? Ever think it would be this huge global phenomenon? How do you guys play it? What strategies do you use? Can you tell us anything about the next versions of the game?*

Soon after that, yet another surprise awaits the team: Steph Curry has followed up his congratulatory Friday night tweets in a big way.

The NBA superstar has sent along new shoes and swag. UMBC wears the Under Armour shoes that Curry reps. So he's gifted them the new, as-yet-unreleased Curry 5's to replace the Curry 4's they wore against Virginia.

"It's like Christmas in March (Madness)!" @ UMBCAthletics tweets as the excited players gather to try on their new kicks. Curry has also sent along the cool warm-up jerseys the team will wear tonight – one of which they'll gift to Cara Jaye – and a personalized note wishing them luck and saying that everyone would be watching tonight as they continue to try to make even more history.

Watching the players admiring their new footwear, Eric Skeeters feels a slight pang of worry.

None of these guys have even practiced in these new shoes, he thinks. Over the years, he's learned that players – and their feet—react differently to new footwear. *It's not like the old days where everyone wears the same shoe, the old Chuck Taylors, and you had a practice pair and a game pair.*

Yet by the time the time the Retrievers arrive at Spectrum Center, video games and new shoes are afterthoughts. Now their focus is on Kansas State. The no. 9 seed from the powerful Big 12 Conference, it's a team hungry to prove itself after going 0-3 in first-round tournament games since 2013.

The Wildcats, 69-59 winners over no. 8 Creighton Friday night, also seem determined to not be another easy mark for the plucky squad that has won the hearts of the nation.

"We know that everyone is kind of looking for that Cinderella story," K-State guard Barry Brown Jr. told reporters a day earlier. Making it clear the Wildcats would like nothing better than to push Cinderella down a flight of stairs.

As the Retrievers clamber off the bus and make their way to the locker room, Ryan Odom wonders if his team will have the legs to compete with K-State after the relentless, up-tempo game the Retrievers played for 40 minutes against Virginia.

He also worries about their ability to score against Kansas State, a team, like Virginia, known for its smothering defense.

The Wildcats' D doesn't have a sexy name attached to it like the Pack Line. But their coach, Bruce Weber, now in his sixth year in Manhattan, sends his team through something called the Rush Drill – which sounds equally unsettling—at every practice.

Essentially, it's a transition defense drill designed to do three things: cover against the deep pass to, guard the ball and cover the first pass up the court. It doesn't take much to set the fiery Weber off. Some of his temper tantrums are legendary. Many are preserved forever in Internet videos eagerly sought out for their vast entertainment value by connoisseurs of coaching flip-outs.

But if you want to *really* see Weber bug out, be the poor guy in the Rush Drill at mid-court who zones out for a second and gives up an easy basket behind him.

Yet even as Odom is impressed with the size and athleticism of the Wildcats, he thinks: *Hey, we can beat them.*

When he looks at his players, he's not seeing an exhausted team. *But after all the celebrating this weekend,* he thinks, *the lack of sleep, the hype and media attention, after seeing ourselves on Sports Center and every other news show a hundred times, do we have enough left in the tank mentally and emotionally for another great performance?*

Against another tough team?

On this kind of stage?

With the whole country watching again?

As game time approaches, though, the players seem unfazed by the challenge before them. Their demeanor, the coaches sense, is no different than it's been before every other game.

This has always been a loose team, a team that likes to laugh and joke around and doesn't take itself too seriously. Since the upset of Virginia, Nate Dixon has been ragging them about their new-found celebrity status. ("Did your third-grade girlfriend who you hadn't talked to in a long time tweet you or text you? Because she saw you on TV?") And it never fails to make them howl with laughter.

But now the joking is over. Instead, there's a calm, business-like air in the locker room, as befits a team eager to prove Friday's win was no fluke.

On the whiteboard, Odom writes: "There's history today. You're 40 minutes away from the Sweet 16."

He also writes down 0-135, then lines out the zero and replaces it with 1. Translation: after 135 previous games, you guys are the first 16-seed ever to play a second-round game. Finally, as he does before every game, he writes 1-0!

The players know what it means. We're not thinking about the game that just happened. We're not worried about the next game. All we care about is going 1-0 today.

"Just be confident," Odom tells his team. "Let's play the way we're capable of playing."

Taking this all in and looking around the room, Jairus Lyles thinks. *We're locked in. We're focused on the new task, that for sure.*

Yet so apparently is Kansas State.

When Eric Skeeters goes out to the court for pre-game warm-ups, he sees the Wildcats' junior guard, Kamau Stokes, putting up shots. Stokes is a Baltimore kid who had a terrific prep career, playing on a City College High School team that went 27-0 and won a state title.

He also played on a state championship team for legendary Dunbar High as a junior, after playing his freshman and sophomore years for Catholic school powerhouse John Carroll High. Yep, the kid has bounced around. But he's tough and resourceful, Skeeters knows, like the gritty city where he grew up.

But now Skeeters attempts a little psychological probing. He wants to see if he can get in the kid's head. So begins a rolling stream of fawning patter to see if Mr. Kamau Stokes is on his game or not.

"Hey man," he tells Stokes, "great job! You're doing a great job!"

Stokes looks at him. No reaction.

"You guys are playing so well!" Skeeters continues. "Take it easy on us today, OK?"

Still no reaction.

But Skeeters is a master at these mind games. He's not about to give up. He was a young assistant to head coach Ron "Fang" Mitchell on the 15-seed Coppin State team that knocked off 2-seed South Carolina in the 1997 tournament.

Like Nate Dixon, he's spent years studying how players react to the enormous pressure of big-time games.

"Hey, where's Coach Frazier?" Skeeters says, referring to K-State assistant coach Chester Frazier, another Baltimore guy who played at perennial power Lake Clifton High and later at Illinois. "Doesn't he come out when you guys warm-up? He's not working you guys out before the game?"

Making it seem like: *Hey, isn't your coach being kind of negligent? Not being out here with you guys? Moments before another huge game? Doesn't he care about you?*

The Wildcats' guard just stares.

Finally he says: "He's in the locker room."

And without another word, he turns and continues shooting.

Ohhh-kay, Skeeters thinks. *Guess we're not the only ones locked in.*

CHAPTER 25

One More Supernatural Performance?

* * * *

Charlotte, N.C.

If UMBC fans are looking for a good omen as the Retrievers take the court, there is this: Charlotte is still the home office for big upsets in this tournament. In fact, Texas A&M has just beaten North Carolina, the no. 2 seed in the West Regional, in the earlier game here.

The no. 7 seed Aggies didn't just squeak by the defending national champions, either. The final score was 86-65, an embarrassing whipping for the defending national champion Tar Heels in what's as close to a home game as they could have.

It's only the second time in 36 NCAA Tournament games in the state of North Carolina that they've lost. And it's the first time in 13 games they've lost a March Madness game in Charlotte.

Adding to their current misery: the school has faced accusations of academic violations amid a lingering NCAA investigation that seems to have gone on forever. No wonder that, as Retriever fans eagerly settle into their seats for the 7:45 p.m. tip-off, they're met by hordes of stone-faced, blue-and-white clad Carolina fans heading for the exits.

Another possible harbinger of good fortune for UMBC: the same broadcasting team behind the microphones for UMBC's upset of Virginia — Jim Nantz and Co.—will call this one for truTV. And as they set the scene for viewers in their opening remarks, they seem even more captivated by the Retrievers than they were two nights earlier.

Sideline reporter Tracy Wolfson, talks about the "crazy 48 hours" the UMBC players have had, going without sleep, having their cell phones blow up, delighting in seeing themselves over and over again on TV.

She also points out that the idea of the Retrievers beating Virginia was initially considered so unthinkable that their parents have had to re-book flights home, "while the kids had to do laundry, because they only brought one change of clothes."

(Laundry, fortunately, would turn out to be an issue mainly for the pep band and dance squad, whose members also converged on the local Target for fresh underwear. Whether due to an unshakeable belief in their team or superior foresight in packing, there were no reports of the Retrievers themselves foraging for quarters and tiny boxes of Tide at the local laundromat.)

When Nantz, Bill Raftery and Grant Hill get around to the subject of Jairus Lyles, all three seem still in awe of how the uber-confident senior guard almost single-handedly destroyed the Cavaliers.

"Twenty-eight points on Friday night," Nantz intones. "It felt like he was never gonna miss."

"One of the most impressive performances I've ever seen in the NCAA Tournament," Hill, the former Duke All-American and NBA All-Star adds. "He carved apart UVA, with the best defense in all of college basketball.

"The question is," Hill continues, "does he have one more supernatural performance in him? Because this team will need it against Kansas State."

In the opening minutes, it appears Lyles is definitely capable of more heroics. Gathering in a long rebound off a three-point attempt by Kamau Stokes, he races the length of the court, does a nifty Euro-step and lays the ball in for the first points of the game.

"And Lyles is *still* hot from Friday night!" Hill exclaims.

Arkel Lamar follows with a three-pointer from the left side of the key. Less than a minute later, Lyles maneuvers around a screen from Joe Sherburne and weaves his way around two defenders for an easy layup to make it 7-0.

Conveniently, K-State is cold as ice, scoreless after eight trips down the court. But for Odom, it's reassuring to see his players bouncing around with such energy, attacking the basket with such vigor.

No dead legs here. At least not yet.

The Wildcats finally score their first basket with 13:39 left − on their 12th trip down the floor—when 6-9 sophomore forward Makol Maiwen takes an entry pass down low and lays it in. But when Jourdan Grant answers with a three from the corner for a 10-2 Retrievers' lead, there's a palpable sense in the UMBC cheering sections that what they're seeing is a repeat of what they saw in the second half Friday night: a team aggressively making shots, running the floor with swagger and playing lock-down defense.

When Lyles leads a fast-break two minutes later and finds Max Curran streaking down the lane for a layup and a 12-6 UMBC lead, Hill marvels: "There was some concern about whether UMBC could bounce back. They look better at the start of this game than they did against Virginia!"

"Anyone goes on the road without clothes, don't count 'em out!" Raftery quips, promulgating the discounted laundry myth that will follow the Retrievers for days.

The sight of Curran—who looks not at all drowsy from his late-night Twitter adventures—out-hustling the Wildcats' defenders for an easy bucket brings the UMBC fans to their feet again. It has the opposite effect on the K-State coaching staff: Bruce Weber wears the look of a man passing a kidney stone.

But Kansas State is not about to panic. This is a team that plays in the Big 12, currently the top-ranked conference in the country, where seemingly every game is a dock brawl. The Wildcats have taken plenty of early shots to the mouth this season and bounced back.

Sure enough, they start finding their rhythm on offense. Finally, at the 8:29 mark, sophomore forward Xavier Sneed steamrolls Jourdan Grant for a layup to give them the lead for the first time, 15-14.

The Retrievers, on the other hand, have been held scoreless the past three minutes. And what follows is some sloppy basketball by both teams, full of turnovers, shots clanging off the rim and air-balls.

But this isn't Saturday at the Y with 10 fat guys heaving passes into the bleachers. It's the tight man-to-man defense of both the Retrievers and Wildcats that's thoroughly disrupting any offensive flow and causing all the chaos.

Kansas State goes up by four on a one-hander off the glass by junior guard Amaad Wainright and a rare mistake by the usually-reliable K.J. Maura. His inbounds pass is stolen by the Wildcats' terrific guard, Barry Brown Jr., who takes it the length of the court for a layup with under five minutes remaining.

But Maura atones for the mistake right away when he drives the lane and hits on a floater to cut the K-State lead to 19-17.

"They need Maura that!" Raftery exclaims.

It's a groaner, for sure. But the sight of the tiny guard charging fearlessly into the paint and making a play energizes the UMBC bench. It gets the Retrievers' fans going, too, as does the sight of Melvin Maura waving the Fathead of his son when it flashes on the video screens.

"Mugsy Bogues!" cries Raftery when Maura's shot is shown on the re-play. "Personifying the little guy with the monster ticker!"

Older viewers get the reference instantly. Tyrone "Mugsy" Bogues, at 5-3, played in the '80's at Wake Forest. He followed that up with a 14-year career in the NBA, despite being the league's shortest player ever.

Raftery's analogy is spot-on and touches on an undeniable truism: a player of Maura's size needs a heart the size of Wyoming to excel at this level.

When K-State's Brown Jr. drops a killer hesitation move on Arkel Lamar and blows by him for an easy layup, the Wildcats have their biggest lead of the half, 23-17, with 2:44 to go. Their clawing, suffocating defense is giving the Retrievers fits now, making them do things they're not comfortable doing.

Joe Sherburne, for example, is normally an excellent catch-and-shoot player, especially when he gets the ball in the right circumstances. But now, feeling the need to make something happen, he puts the ball on the floor, drives the lane, spins and puts up a fade-away jumper over K-State guard Cartier Diarra.

But the shot caroms harmlessly off the front of the rim, making Sherburne 0-for-5 from the floor and deepening the frustration for the Retrievers.

A Brown jumper seconds later ups the K-State lead to 25-17. Meanwhile, UMBC's scoring the rest of the way will consist of only three free throws from Jourdan Grant, one of the lone Retrievers still attacking the basket.

Jairus Lyles, the hero of the past two games, is another Retriever who seems out of sync, a far cry from the unassailable scoring machine he's been.

In the waning seconds, he takes a long jumper from three feet beyond the arc that misses. And his driving left-hand layup right before the horn sounds caroms high off the glass, bounces to the floor and goes out of bounds, making him 2-for-8 from the floor.

But as they jog off the court at halftime and glance up at the scoreboard, the Retrievers take some solace in what they see.

They know they haven't played horribly. But they also know they haven't played anywhere near their capabilities. And they trail by only five, 25-20.

With a whole lot of game to go.

This dock brawl, they feel, is just getting started.

CHAPTER 26

A Legacy in the Balance

• • • •

Charlotte, N.C.

In the Retrievers' locker room, there is no mystery as to why they're trailing. A look at the stat sheet tells the story in stark and simple terms.

Kansas State is getting too many points (16) inside. In Ryan Odom's mind, the Wildcats have been more aggressive going high-low than Virginia was. And the Retrievers aren't making their shots. They shot 29 per cent from the floor for the first half. They were 2-for-9 from three-point range. They were 4-for-9 from the foul line.

Open looks have been hard to find. K-State is switching on defense and it's bothering UMBC. The Wildcats held Creighton to a season-low 33 per cent Friday. But even when the Retrievers get an open shot, the ball isn't going down. And this is normally a good-shooting team.

Jairus Lyles hasn't made a basket since five minutes into the game. He missed his last five shots. And Joe Sherburne still hasn't scored, period.

Not that K-State is exactly burning the nets from the outside, either. The Wildcats' field goal percentage was only 38. And they were 0-for-8 in three pointers. But they've been disruptive on defense, scoring seven points off turnovers to none for UMBC.

Like all veteran coaches, Odom has a favorite halftime spiel he trots out, which can be relevant in multiple scenarios.

If UMBC has a big lead, he'll often tell the players: "Fellas, I've never seen a team win a game at halftime." Meaning: don't relax, we still have plenty of work to do. But the beauty of this line is, he can pretty much use it if his team is behind, too.

But he doesn't use the line now. That's because the Retrievers themselves seem unconcerned about being down five points. All season long, this is a team that has always had confidence in itself. Odom senses zero doubt in the room now.

So as his players prepare to take the floor for the second half, Odom tells them: "Hey, if we go out there and play a great half and really guard them and get our offense going – and our offense *is* going to get going – we're going to the Sweet 16."

Odom wants more penetration, more kick-out passes, better ball movement. It wouldn't hurt to have K-State fall asleep on defense, either. And that's what happens in the opening minutes when Dan Akin slips behind a wall of Wildcat defenders down low and Lyles finds him for an easy lay-in.

Cartier Diarra hits a step-back three for K-State's first points from behind the arc. But the Wildcats fail to rotate on defense once again and Maura hits a wide-open three to pull the Retrievers to within 28-25 approaching the 17-minute mark.

It sets off spate of goofy Fortnite dances led by Nolan Gerrity and his pals on the UMBC bench, and now there's a sense the Retrievers are emerging from their offensive doldrums. When Gerrity checks into the game moments later, Nantz says: "I guess he showed Coach Odom something with that dance move! Put that energy on the floor!"

But Raftery, the Jersey wise-guy, has a different—more darkly biting—take on why Odom subbed in his blond-haired, wildly-gyrating forward: "I think he was tired of looking at it! (He thought) 'Get out there and play!'"

When Jourdan Grant blocks a jumper by Barry Brown and Max Curran hits a three seconds later to trim the K-State lead to 32-31, it sounds as if the entire building is cheering for the Retrievers.

And when Maura draws an offensive foul on the Wildcats next trip down the court and K-State's big man Makol Marwein picks up his third foul seconds later and heads to the bench, the din grows even louder.

Now it's at ear-bleed levels. "You can feel the energy, the momentum here picking up!" Grant Hill shouts.

Yet the frenetic pace appears to be taking a toll on a few of the Retrievers.

K.J. Maura, uncharacteristically, turns the ball over a couple of times. And he's taken a couple of ill-advised shots. This is the player teammates swear never, ever gets tired. This is their human Energizer Bunny.

After the most grueling of practices, the most draining of games, this is the player most apt to stroll into the locker room looking as if he's been sitting on a beach with a cold drink the past two hours.

Nevertheless, Odom senses the kid needs a rest.

Sometimes you need a blow not only to catch your breath, but to get your mind right and head back in there, Odom thinks.

Sherburne's shooting touch is still missing, too. And with a little over seven minutes to play, Lyles has still not attempted a shot in the half.

On the other hand, it's not as if he's not contributing. The UMBC captain is still racing all over the court. He's rebounding, making slick no-look passes and playing stellar defense. But he seems content to play the role of facilitator on offense, even though it's clear UMBC needs him to attack the basket and score.

"Lyles has gotta go a little more if he's OK, huh?" Raftery observes quietly.

But Lyles is OK. He's not injured. He's not cramping up and serial-licking peanut butter crackers, the way he did two nights ago. In any event, Odom elects to say nothing to his star guard. He doesn't have to. The rest of the UMBC players are in Lyles' ear, urging him to be more active, to get back to being the fabled ISO-Jairus, the king of one-on-one matchups, step-back jumpers and swooping drives to the hole.

With a little over nine minutes left and UMBC trailing by a point while giving K-State all it can handle, Nantz feels the need to remind his broadcast partners that this is the same Retrievers team that lost by 44 to Albany less than two months ago. ("Great Danes Maul Retrievers" was one of the more canine-centric headlines to emerge from that ugly affair.)

"Had to be the flu," Raftery says of UMBC getting blown out.

But Nantz quickly shoots down that notion.

"Everyone was healthy!" he continues. And here are the Retrievers after that terrible beat-down, he marvels, having knocked off the overall no. 1 seed in the tournament and going nose-to-nose with a powerful Big 12 team!

Two free throws by Mawein and a jump shot at the buzzer by Kamau Stokes ups K-State's lead to 38-33 with under seven minutes to play. But it's at this point that Lyles appears to rouse himself.

He's fouled by Brown on a drive to the basket with 6:52 left and makes one of two free throws. And seconds later he hits a long three from behind the arc to again pull the Retrievers to within a point of K-State.

It's Lyles' first basket of the second half. In fact, it's his first basket since the first five minutes of the game. Yet the jab step he uses to get separation from Barry Brown Jr., the ball leaving his hands at the apex of his jump and rotating perfectly on just the right arc to the basket—all of it evokes the Lyles heroics of another do-or-die situation eight days earlier.

"Hello, Vermont!" Raftery exclaims. "From the same spot!"

"Yep," Nantz agrees. It's the shot, he notes, now being called the greatest in UMBC history.

Spectrum Center is rocking again as UMBC fans break into the familiar, hypnotic chant of "Ohh, oh-OH-oh-oh-ohhh-ohhh," from the White Stripes' "Seven Nation Army," the song that's become a sport anthem around the world.

But the momentum lasts only seconds. On UMBC's next possession, Arkel Lamar has the ball stolen by Xavier Sneed, who goes the length of the floor for a thunderous dunk. And when Brown hits a jumper from 14 feet off a high-screen-and-roll to put K-State up 42-37 with a little over four minutes left, it's the Wildcats fans in their royal purple T-shirts whooping and doing line dances in their seats.

They're boogying again a minute later when Sneed seems to leap into the rafters before returning to the mezzanine level to snatch a Brown miss out of the air and slam it home for a six-point K-State lead. And now, for the first time all game, it feels as if this is too much of a gap for an obviously-tired UMBC to overcome.

The Retrievers pull to within 44-41 with a little over two minutes left when the indefatigable Lyles drives the lane, switches hands and puts up a pretty left-handed layup. But a 10-foot jumper by Sneed and a dunk by Mawein after the Wildcats break the Retrievers' press gives K-State a 48-41 lead with 40 seconds to go.

When Joe Sherburne misses an easy layup off a gorgeous pass from Maura with 33 seconds remaining, a sense of the inevitable finally overcomes the Retrievers. Heads bow and shoulders sag as they shuffle wearily to the other end of the court after Lyles is forced to foul Brown.

When Odom subs out all five players so UMBC fans can acknowledge them for the final time, it sets off a weepy conga line on the bench of players hugging teammates and coaches. And in the ultimate sign of respect, even the K-State supporters join in the ovation.

This time, a downcast K.J. Maura doesn't shoot any imaginary love arrows into the stands. Instead he stares up at his family and says: "Sorry."

"It's OK!" his father Melvin shouts in Spanish. "You have done so much!"

The final score is 50-43. And after the horn sounds and the two teams shake hands, the UMBC fans give the Retrievers a standing ovation. Nantz's send-off is heart-felt: "The biggest Cinderella in the history of the tournament walks off the floor in Charlotte, making another memorable statement about effort here."

In the opening minutes of the truTV post-game show, Ernie Johnson also seems obliged to speak to UMBC's grit, and to the legacy the gutty Retrievers have carved out this weekend.

"It was only one game," Johnson says. "But it doesn't take long to capture the imagination of an entire viewing public . . . The name will forever be remembered, whether it's shows like this or 'Jeopardy' or *somewhere*."

Sitting in front of his laptop before the arena goes dark, Zach Seidel, the social media maven, attempts to author a fitting coda for the incredible March Madness weekend the Retrievers have experienced.

In a few moments, a student assistant will mosey over to him and, in an attempt to be comforting, say: "You're a legend at school now."

Legend, schmegend, Seidel thinks.

He doesn't care about any of that now. Brow furrowed, eyes narrowed in concentration as he stares at the screen, he's trying to summon the muse. Trying to *create* something.

Finally, his fingers lower to the keyboard and this is the message that goes out from the @UMBCAthletics to the tens of thousands of new followers the site has amassed over the past three wonderful, chaotic and inspiring days:

"Well, it was fun, y'all. K-State may have won. But we hope to have won your hearts."

CHAPTER 27

A Surreal Feel To It All

• • • •

Charlotte, N.C.

The end of a college basketball season is always an abrupt, mournful affair.

Only one team, the one that hoists the championship trophy in April and cuts down the nets as "One Shining Moment" blares in the background, is ever truly satisfied with what it has achieved. For every other team, the realization of having no more games – and having fallen short of goals—is jarring and depressing.

In the quiet Retrievers locker room, Ryan Odom moves to the whiteboard and writes the word "Proud" before addressing his players.

As is his custom after every season, he talks about the seniors who have played their last game for UMBC, in this case Jairus Lyles, K.J. Maura and Jourdan Grant. He talks about what each player has meant, not just to him, but to the UMBC program.

He talks about how proud he is of each of them, and how far each has come since he first took over as coach two years earlier. And he talks about how much he appreciated Lyles and Grant staying on when they could have fled the sinking ship that was UMBC hoops back then to play elsewhere.

Odom has a particular soft spot for the affable Grant, the lone four-year senior on the team and a player his coach calls a "Swiss army knife" because of his versatility. This is the kid who suffered through truly miserable 4-26 and 7-25 seasons before Odom came aboard, then lost his starting role when Maura joined the team.

Odom knew that could have been an issue. A sulking, griping Grant would have been poison for a new coach trying to instill a winning culture. Instead, the kid put his personal feeling aside and embraced his sixth man/defensive specialist role.

Not only that, but like something out of a Hollywood buddy movie or a corny sitcom, he went on to become best friends with the guy who replaced him as a starter. Ever since, Odom has always cited him as a shining example of a player who truly sacrificed for his team.

Talking about him now, there's a lump in Odom's throat. He's starting to miss the kid already.

When the coach is through lauding each senior, he tells them: "You'll always be one of us. You'll never have to ask to come home."

Now everyone in the room is emotional. And as Odom watches the rest of his players hugging the seniors one-by-one, he's tearing up, too.

How could he not?

It's Odom's firm belief that each season, the group of people that come together as a team—coaches, players, staff members, trainers – has *one* chance to do something special with that group. Because *that* group will never exist again in the same way.

Next year, there will be new people in the group, certainly new players, and maybe new coaches, too, if the losses pile up and the administration and alums get antsy. These days, coaches get tossed aside like old Tupperware if they don't win out of the gate.

Who knows that better than Odom, the basketball lifer whose dad was a basketball lifer, too? And what he knows is that this group, these gritty players who will be part of NCAA lore forever, will no longer be a part of *his* life in quite the same way after tonight.

"Hey, you left it out there," he tells them. "You'll have a memory that will last a lifetime. You guys will forever be connected. Thirty years from now, you'll be able to reminisce. You'll remember the (Virginia) win, obviously. But you'll remember the times together that you were able to experience. The fun times. And the hard times too."

There is, to be sure, a lot of soul-searching going on in the room, too.

Maybe it was too much for the Retrievers to think they could again play up to the sublime level they reached against Virginia. But they know that just playing a little bit better tonight – coupled with a few breaks—might have been enough to land in the Sweet 16.

Instead, the Retrievers turned the ball over 17 times. They were 6-for-22 from beyond the three-point line. They were just 9-for-18 from the free throw line. They had 18 chances in the second half to take the lead.

Jairus Lyles, the stalwart playmaker all year, finished 4-for-15 from the field with 12 points. And the normally-reliable Joe Sherburne missed on all nine of his shot attempts, many of them open looks.

"It was my worst game of the season," Sherburne will say. And *still*, despite all of it, UMBC was in the game until the very end.

Yet even amid the gloom that hangs over them, some of the Retrievers are also choosing to remind themselves of the positives that came out of this wild, tumultuous weekend in North Carolina.

They had played their hearts out as huge underdogs in both games, and brought an out-sized level of pride to their fans, their school and their conference.

"When you're in a smaller conference like we are," Sherburne tells reporters, "you see a lot of talk about 'These small conferences shouldn't even be in the tournament,' We don't need 16-seeds.' So obviously I think we changed some people's minds."

They had also, of course, made history on a glorious night at Spectrum Center. They had beaten the no. 1 team in all the land, transfixed hoops fans everywhere and become America's team. All of that could never be taken away from them.

Nor could the enormous satisfaction K.J. Maura feels as the newest hero for the height-challenged everywhere.

"I got a lot of messages from little kids," he tells the media, brightening. "They said I gave them strength and hope to follow their dreams. That makes my heart warm."

CHAPTER 28

Lots of Love in the Air

• • • •

Catonsville, Md.

After the short flight to BWI-Marshall airport, the UMBC bus, complete with a police escort, arrives back on campus at a little after 2 in the morning.

Spring break is still on, the university windswept and largely deserted. But there, waiting in the cold and the inky darkness to welcome them back, are some three dozen students and fans.

The small crowd cheers wildly as the groggy players and coaches climb off the bus one by one. At first the Retrievers seem stunned to find anyone but themselves awake and moving about at this ungodly hour.

When reserve forward Brandon Horvath sees students joyously recording the scene on their iPhones and shouting "We love you guys!" he stares uncomprehendingly, as if a terrible mistake has been made and all these people are in the wrong place.

But eventually it dawns on the Retrievers that this gathering is all for them, and the uncertain looks turn to smiles and waves.

"We love you, K.J." the crowd screams when it spots the diminutive guard.

Oh, yes, there's a lot of love in the air. In response, Maura mimics shooting one of his arrows, then goes over to talk to the happy throng. Fans showing up in the dead of night to show their support for the basketball team – it's something he could never have envisioned even a few weeks ago.

"It feels so surreal," he tells a local TV reporter. Yet it's indicative, he continues, of the "changes in the culture at UMBC. It's a great feeling."

Among the frozen die-hards greeting the team is Corey Johns, a 2011 UMBC grad who is clapping so hard his hands are starting to sting. The 28-year-old is a huge March Madness junkie; seeing his beloved school make such a splash this past weekend in such an elevated setting has left him ecstatic.

Like so many UMBC alums his age, though, the Retrievers have also caused him a fair amount of pain over the years.

All the losing back in the day was soul-crushing. He can flash back to a particularly horrid game in 2015, the infamous 4-26 season. This was Jourdan Grant's first year. There was, as usual, no one in the stands that night, the Retrievers inspiring a huge collective yawn among the student body. And for this one game, the team was down to six or seven players because of injuries.

It got so bad that the team manager was pressed into filling a roster spot. And it felt like if anyone else went down, they were going to have to throw a uniform at the startled kid working the concession stand and bark: "OK, put down those Junior Mints and suit up."

But now, three years later, Johns sees a brighter future for UMBC basketball. When Ryan Odom finally gets off the bus, he receives the loudest ovation of all. And when he walks over to Johns and the others and thanks them for their support, someone shouts: "Coach of the Year!"

Odom shakes his head.

"Players of the Year!" he says softly. Then: "Will you come out to see us next year?"

Now another animated cheer goes up and Corey Johns smiles.

He's a bail bondsman now, but his connection to the school feels stronger than ever. He'll definitely come out to watch the Retrievers next year. And he's willing to bet lots of other people will, too, and that the UMBC Event Center will be rocking when they again take the court in November.

Sure, he knows there are no guarantees that next season turns out anything like this one. After all, the team will be losing three key seniors, including the great Lyles, the very heart and soul of the Retrievers. The one player you couldn't take your eyes off all year long, the one who seems most irreplaceable.

But it's also a team, Johns feels, with a smart young coach who knows how to win—and can get his players to believe they can win, too.

For now, Johns knows, it's a team that mesmerized a nation and made history in the most improbable fashion on an electric March night in North Carolina. And who's to say it can't make even more history in the years to come?

EPILOGUE

●●●●

The days that follow are heady ones for Retriever Nation.

A little over a week after the team's remarkable odyssey in Charlotte, Freeman Hrabowski's fear of losing Ryan Odom to a Power Five school vanishes. Rumored to be the "hot" coach of the moment, with dozens of teams interested in talking with him, Odom puts all the speculation to rest and agrees to new contract with UMBC.

Details emerging later show that the revised deal nearly doubles his base salary from $225,000 to $425,000, with other lucrative incentive clauses thrown in. From all indications, the school is thrilled to pay it.

"There's been a real paradigm shift in the way kids are," athletic director Tim Hall tells USA Today about the push to re-sign Odom. "Back when we played, if a coach said 'Run through that wall,' you'd say 'How fast?' Kids aren't like that today.

"(Ryan) just has a great way of explaining context, getting kids to understand the why and then building belief. He gets kids to believe they're better than they are."

Hours later, the team is feted by Gov. Larry Hogan and other dignitaries at a ceremony at the governor's mansion in Annapolis. Hogan is a rabid fan. He was also a true believer in this team from the moment it punched its ticket to March Madness.

A day before the upset of Virginia, the Republican governor had tweeted out his brackets. Not only did he have the no. 16 Retrievers beating the no. 1 Cavaliers, but he had them beating no. 9 Kansas State, going all the way to the Final Four and then beating Michigan in the national championship game.

When news of Odom's new pact with the school is announced at the reception, it's Hogan who pumps his fists, cheers and appears to be the happiest person in the room.

With the Retrievers noshing on appetizers and gazing around in wonder at their stately surroundings, Hogan presents them with a handsome plaque noting their achievements and a special governor's coin, a coveted piece of political swag. Later, the team is also recognized on the floor of both the state Senate and House of Delegates.

The following night, the Retrievers are honored in an hour-long campus celebration in the new Event Center. Billed grandly as a party for "our conquering heroes," it takes place on a day proclaimed as "UMBC Making History Day" by Baltimore County officials.

Hrabowski's announcement to the spirited crowd that Odom will be staying on draws a sustained roar, as does another of his observations: "We have never had a more celebrated period in the history of UMBC!"

Afterward, lines of fans holding all manner of team apparel, posters and memorabilia snake through the arena seeking autographs – and selfies—from the UMBC players and coaches.

In early April, beating out 21 other finalists, Odom is named the Hugh Durham National Coach of the Year, given annually to the mid-majors' top coach. Later that month, he throws out the ceremonial first pitch at Camden Yards before the Orioles game against the Cleveland Indians.

In a chat with O's Hall of Famer Jim Palmer before he takes the mound, Odom is given invaluable advice: whatever you do, *don't* throw from the pitching rubber. Throw from well in front of it. Otherwise, you'll corkscrew yourself into the ground, bounce the ball 15 feet in front of the plate and look like a doofus in front of everyone here and on TV.

The tip pays off. With his smiling players arrayed behind him, all wearing special Retriever-gold Orioles caps, Odom shows off an abbreviated windup, decent velocity and excellent location, hitting the outside corner of the plate.

With the Orioles mired in a six-game losing streak, his performance prompts a number of snarky tweets urging the O's front office to sign the UMBC coach since, as one fan puts it, "He's better than anyone we've got in the rotation."

"Can he give us five good innings?" another fan wonders on-line.

At the end of the month, the Retrievers make the venerable New York Times crossword puzzle. (The clue is: UMBC over Virginia e.g. The solution is: upset.) And in

May comes the ultimate affirmation that the Retrievers have officially ingrained themselves into the world of pop culture: they're getting their own bobblehead.

The National Bobblehead Hall of Fame and Museum – who knew such a thing existed? – releases the rendering of the figurine commemorating the team's stunning upset of Virginia. It depicts a cartoonish True Grit, the school's trusty mascot, standing on a stack of newspapers, one blaring the front page headline: "UMBC Does the Unthinkable! #16 Topples #1 for 1st Time in Men's Tourney."

The scowling T. Grit also holds a sign that says: "U Must Be Cinderella." The bobbleheads will sell for $35. Each will come in a collector's box.

Despite all the hype and hoopla, for Ryan and Lucia Odom, the weeks following the "Shocker in Charlotte" are by no means carefree. Within days after UMBC's loss to Kansas State, it's obvious that their son, Connor, is spiraling down once more with his OCD.

This time, though, there is no return to the hospital in Nashville. Connor's symptoms are serious, but not quite as severe as before. In the words of his mother Lucia, "he was staying afloat, he wasn't going under."

Connor opts to try to beat the illness himself. A transfer to a new school, the prep basketball powerhouse Oak Hill Academy in Virginia, gives him a new focus and helps to ease his depression.

It's a lonely battle, fighting this latest bout with the illness. But his perseverance and determination not to give in to it inspires his family. And months later, when Connor is finally feeling better, Ryan Odom will take his son aside and tell him: "I've never been prouder of you than I am right now."

In the weeks after re-writing NCAA Tournament history, UMBC is also feeling the "Flutie Effect." Named after Doug Flutie, the Boston College quarterback whose last-second "Hail Mary" touchdown pass beat Miami in the 1984 Orange Bowl, it refers to the exposure and benefits a university reaps after it pulls off a stunning upset on national TV.

UMBC cashes in big-time as a result of its upset for the ages in Charlotte: an estimated $20 million in free marketing, a huge spike in gifts from donors, a lucrative run on Retrievers apparel and merchandise sales in the team store, a big increase in attendance at campus visit events for prospective students and an uptick in freshman enrollment. (A corporate sponsor for the Event Center, on the other hand, still has not materialized.)

Over 4,700 articles in publications such as The New York Times, Washington Post, USA Today, Forbes and Sports Illustrated mention UMBC's March Madness win and lead to the kind of "brand advertising" many schools can only dream of. Traffic to umbc.edu also more than quadruples.

Dr. Freeman Hrabowski, the school's tireless John the Baptist, senses a new-found pride in the student body, as well as a belief that there's more campus life than originally thought. He also feels that, corporate sponsor or no, the new 5,000-seat, $85-million on-campus arena will become a transformative symbol of a university striving to shed its stodgy, nose-to-the-grindstone image as No Fun U.

In the midst of this exhilarating time, there are also those inevitable moments when UMBC's players are humbled, when they come face-to-face with the realization that not everyone on the planet has been fixated on their grand post-season journey.

One of those moments occurs with the promised national roll-out of Little Caesars' "Free lunch combo if crazy happens." The "crazy," of course, was a 16-seed knocking off a 1 in March Madness. The promotion is a huge success; news programs report on long lines of pizza lovers at affiliates all over the country eager to take advantage of the deal.

When Joe Sherburne and a couple of teammates show up for their four slices of deep-dish pepperoni and a 20-oz. soda, the line outside the store appears to stretch to Pennsylvania. Sherburne is running late for class. So rather than wait, he and his buddies devise an alternative strategy.

But as he tells the Baltimore Sun: " . . . We tried to walk to the front of the line and be like 'We're the reason you're getting free pizza.' And, like, five per cent of the line knew why there was free pizza.'"

"I think I kind of learned throughout this that people don't know sports as much as you think they do," Nolan Gerrity tells the newspaper.

Zach Seidel experiences one of those humbling moments, too. A couple of months later, he's with the school's women's volleyball team at Penn State. Everyone is clad in Retrievers gear when a woman approaches and says: "UMBC? What's that?"

"University of Maryland, Baltimore County," Seidel answers. "We're the school that beat Virginia in the NCAA Tournament."

"Huh," the woman says blankly.

"You didn't hear about that?" Seidel asks.

The woman shakes her head no. And in a tone of voice Seidel found more than a little condescending, she adds: "Good for you!" before walking away.

God, Seidel thinks, *I hope we KILL Penn State in volleyball today.*

In June, the Retrievers are nominated for "Best Moment" in the 2018 ESPY Awards that celebrate "major sports achievements, reliving unforgettable moments and saluting the leading performers and performances."

Ryan Odom and players K.J Maura, Joe Sherburne, Jourdan Grant, Arkel Lamar, Nolan Gerrity and Max Curran fly out to Los Angeles for the glitzy awards ceremony the following month. (Jairus Lyles, prepping for a shot with the NBA, does not make the trip.)

After walking the red carpet that night, they excitedly take their seats in the darkened Microsoft Theater. All of them, including long-time SID Steve Levy, are convinced UMBC will win. Odom, who has prepared an acceptance speech, confesses to having butterflies, certain he'll soon be addressing the droves of big-time jocks and celebrities in the crowd, as well as a national television audience.

No wonder the Retrievers think they're a shoo-in to win. After all, two of the other "Best Moment" nominees are Notre Dame over Mississippi State to win the NCAA women's hoop tournament and the Las Vegas Golden Knights besting the Winnipeg Jets in the NHL Stanley Cup playoffs.

Tremendous accomplishments, sure. *But c'mon*, the Retrievers think, *what sports moment could possibly top what we did?*

Two-thirds of the way through the program, they get their answer: *The Espy for 2018 Best Moment goes to . . . the Minnesota Vikings!* It's for the Vikes' stunning "Minneapolis Miracle" in the NFC divisional playoff, when, on the last play of the game, Stefon Diggs hauled in a 61-yard touchdown pass from quarterback Case Keenum for a 29-24 win over the New Orleans Saints.

The Retrievers are definitely bummed. They mutter dark oaths to each other and slump lower in their seats. For Joe Sherburne, however, the night isn't a total loss: he finally gets to meet his long-time idol. Spotting Aaron Rodgers in one of the front rows – the star quarterback's girlfriend, Danica Patrick, is hosting – Sherburne waits for a break in the action and introduces himself.

And soon he gets the memento of a lifetime: a glossy photo of himself with the Green Bay Packers great, the two of them beaming like they're old fraternity brothers.

For the Virginia coaches and players, the weeks after losing to UMBC are a far more unsettling and melancholy time.

Despite Tony Bennett delivering some of the most gracious and inspiring post-game remarks of all time, despite the Virginia coaches and players taking responsibility for the shocking loss and vowing to grow from it, the crazies come out howling, as they always do after upsets like this one.

Bennett and his players are ripped on social media. They're targeted with death threats. They're told they're a national embarrassment. Bennett's methodical offense is mocked and criticized relentlessly.

All the stress leads their terrific guard, Kyle Guy, to open up about the disabling anxiety attacks he's been having all season, which were made worse after losing to UMBC. He talks about the pain he's felt, about having to take medication for his issues, about seeing a sports psychologist.

By going public, Guy says, he hopes his story can help others with similar problems.

Reading about the Virginia star's struggles months later, Ryan Odom immediately empathizes, given all that Connor has dealt with for years. With the Cavaliers in the midst of another excellent season and vying for another Final Four berth, the UMBC coach sends a heartfelt, hand-written letter to Guy, praising his courage in speaking out.

What the young man is offering others, Odom tells the Virginia Pilot, is hope.

"You're providing (it to) somebody else that is really struggling – there's another Kyle Guy out there, another Connor Odom out there . . ." Odom says. "You . . . might provide that youngster with some hope that he needs at that particular time, and you don't even know you're doing it."

Seeing a letter from UMBC, Guy assumed at first it would be hate mail – or worse. The nutjobs put poison in envelopes these days, don't they? But after reading it, he was moved.

"Class act," he says of Odom to the newspaper. "He's a high-character guy."

Just days later, Virginia beats Texas Tech 85-77 in an overtime thriller for its first national championship. And leaping into the air at the final buzzer and shooting a triumphant fist to the heavens, a beaming Kyle Guy looks like the happiest man on the planet.

"I'm back to the old me," he tells everyone.

Just one year after the lowest low of their careers, Bennett and his players have reached the highest high. And in the post-game presser, Bennett talks about how the searing loss to UMBC, which unmoored his team at first, eventually pulled it together and made it stronger.

"If you learn to use it right, "Bennett tells reporters, "the adversity will buy you a ticket to a place you couldn't have gone any other way."

For veteran broadcaster Jim Nantz, what happened on the night of March 16, 2018 in Charlotte was something he'd dreamed of being a part of for years – and something he'll never forget.

"It was a thrill to be able to call the first ever 16 over a 1," he says many months later, happily reliving UMBC's upset for the ages with a writer. "It was such a big part of the history of the tournament. It was such a dominating second-half performance, and so it didn't feel as Cinderella-esque as it would have if they'd won on a buzzer-beater. I don't know if that makes any sense.

"When you win by 20, it was such a thorough victory that by the end, the call is not as iconic as it would have been if it had been a pulsating-type game. . . . The magnitude of that win was certainly enriched by Virginia winning the national championship the next year. It took the UMBC upset to another level, if that's possible.

"It was," he says of the Retrievers, "just a magical team."

To this day, Freeman Hrabowski, when the need strikes him, will pull out his cell phone and watch the play that started the whole wild, improbable journey to Charlotte: the dramatic, last-second Jairus Lyles game-winner in the musty old gym in Burlington.

"Sometimes when I'm feeling discouraged, I'll watch that and derive inspiration," he says. "Every time I watch it, it says: we can do this. When all the odds are against us and the whole world says 'impossible,' we can *do* this!"

About the Author

• • • •

Kevin Cowherd is the *New York Times* best-selling author of "Hothead" and five other baseball novels for young readers written with Hall of Famer Cal Ripken Jr. Cowherd's last work of non-fiction, "When the Crowd Didn't Roar: How Baseball's Strangest Game Ever Gave a Broken City Hope," was praised in the *Times'* 2019 Summer Reading Issue as one of the five best new sports books.

Cowherd was an award-winning sport columnist and features writer for the *Baltimore Sun* for 32 years. He has also written for *Men's Health*, *Parenting* and *Baseball Digest* magazines.

Index

235

Apprentice
House Press
Loyola University Maryland

Apprentice House is the country's only campus-based, student-staffed book publishing company. Directed by professors and industry professionals, it is a nonprofit activity of the Communication Department at Loyola University Maryland.

Using state-of-the-art technology and an experiential learning model of education, Apprentice House publishes books in untraditional ways. This dual responsibility as publishers and educators creates an unprecedented collaborative environment among faculty and students, while teaching tomorrow's editors, designers, and marketers.

Eclectic and provocative, Apprentice House titles intend to entertain as well as spark dialogue on a variety of topics. Financial contributions to sustain the press's work are welcomed. Contributions are tax deductible to the fullest extent allowed by the IRS.

To learn more about Apprentice House books or to obtain submission guidelines, please visit www.apprenticehouse.com.

Apprentice House
Communication Department
Loyola University Maryland
4501 N. Charles Street
Baltimore, MD 21210
Ph: 410-617-5265
info@apprenticehouse.com • www.apprenticehouse.com